Angels Watching Over Me

Angels Watching Over Me

An Extraordinary Investigation into Experiences
of Afterlife Communication

Jacky Newcomb

HAY HOUSE

Australia • Canada • Hong Kong
South Africa • United Kingdom • United States

First published and distributed in the United Kingdom by:
Hay House UK Ltd, 292B Kensal Rd, London W10 5BE. Tel.: (44) 20 8962 1230;
Fax: (44) 20 8962 1239. www.hayhouse.co.uk

Published and distributed in the United States of America by:
Hay House, Inc., PO Box 5100, Carlsbad, CA 92018-5100. Tel.: (1) 760 431 7695 or
(800) 654 5126; Fax: (1) 760 431 6948 or (800) 650 5115. www.hayhouse.com

Published and distributed in Australia by:
Hay House Australia Ltd, 18/36 Ralph St, Alexandria NSW 2015. Tel.: (61) 2 9669 4299;
Fax: (61) 2 9669 4144. www.hayhouse.com.au

Published and distributed in the Republic of South Africa by:
Hay House SA (Pty), Ltd, PO Box 990, Witkoppen 2068. Tel./Fax: (27) 11 467 8904.
www.hayhouse.co.za

Published and distributed in India by:
Hay House Publishers India, Muskaan Complex, Plot No.3, B-2, Vasant Kunj, New Delhi –
110 070. Tel.: (91) 11 4176 1620; Fax: (91) 11 4176 1630. www.hayhouse.co.in

Distributed in Canada by:
Raincoast, 9050 Shaughnessy St, Vancouver, BC V6P 6E5. Tel.: (1) 604 323 7100;
Fax: (1) 604 323 2600

A catalogue record for this book is available from the British Library.

ISBN 978-1-4019-1582-7

Printed in the UK by CPI Bookmarque, Croydon, CR0 4TD

For all the angels in my life: my husband John,
daughters Charlotte and Georgina, and cat
companions Tigger and Magik

I don't believe in the afterlife, but I am bringing along a change of underwear just in case.
WOODY ALLEN

It's my Time

Where do we go when it's time to leave?
It's my time.
Through the tunnel of light, where it's clear and bright.
It's my time.
My friends are all waiting on the other side,
I'm a little bit scared, but my angel's at my side.
It's my time.

I know you'll cry,
But it's my time.
I know you'll be wondering 'Why, why, why?'
But it's my time.
I can't stay on Earth where my work is done.
Heaven is great, I'm happy and it's fun.
It's my time.

I'll always love you and you'll always love me,
But it's my time.
Never forget me, but I want you to move on,
'Coz it's my time.
All good things must come to an end,
You're in my heart, and you'll always be my friend,
But it's my time.

Although we must part it's only for a while.
It's not your time.
Make me proud as you carry on.
It's not your time.

I'll wait for you till you're old and grey,
I'm sorry that you have to stay.
It's not your time.

Life is precious and although it's not the same,
It's not your time.
Life will go on, I think you'll find,
It's not your time.
I want you to promise that while I am away
You'll love one another. I hope and pray ... you'll
understand, my darling,
It's my time, it's my time ... it's my time.

JACKY NEWCOMB

Contents

Acknowledgements

A very big thank you to everyone who shared their stories for the book.

I should also like to thank my editor Lizzie Hutchins, and Michelle Pilley, Jo Burgess, Jo Lal and everyone else at Hay House for their faith in me!

INTRODUCTION

A Spiritual Journey

I have good hope that there is something after death.

PLATO

'Tonight's discussion is about Tony Blair. What are your feelings about the fact that the UK Prime Minister is giving up his post? Call us and have your say,' the radio announcer encouraged. 'Also on tonight's show we have the Angel Lady, Jacky Newcomb. Do you believe in angels or do you think it's a load of rubbish? Ring in and tell us what you think…'

I am regularly invited to chat on radio shows up and down the country. Sometimes I have to drive to the studio and other times I can chat live on the telephone from my bedroom at home. Of course that's the easiest!

'If you have questions or stories about angels and you want to share them with Jacky, ring in on the usual number. You may have to be patient, though; currently all of our phone lines are engaged. Tonight everyone wants to talk about their angels. You can also text in your questions on your mobile phones...'

The first caller was already on the line. 'If you have a light around you, you have an angel on your shoulder, Nicksy,' they explained to the DJ.

Then the next caller came through. 'My granddad died and that night he came to me in a dream and told me not to worry about my driving test the next day. He told me I would pass and get 30 points...' The caller admitted that he did indeed pass his driving test the next day and pick up 30 points.

Another caller explained that her husband had died just a year ago but he visited her and her young daughter, aged three, most nights. The daughter seemed aware of her father's visits and chatted to him as if he were physically in the room.

And so the calls went on, call after call, question after question.

The presenter was really enjoying the phone-in. He asked me if I could stay on later. 'You're bigger than Tony Blair. No one wants to talk about the Prime Minister tonight. We'll have to have you on the radio all day – can you come to Manchester?' He was even gracious enough to share a positive paranormal experience of his own.

The subject of the radio interview was very familiar to me. Thousands and thousands of people have seen their guardian angels and their deceased loved ones. Many of them were interested in ringing in and chatting about their experiences, and I loved it!

So many people all over the world are having encounters with loved ones who have passed on and there is a craving for information. Was it real? Can our loved ones really visit us? Can they give us signs?

I know they can and yet I still queried it myself! 'If this is real, then give me a sign,' I challenged, looking up to the sky. 'Show me that you're here. How about making a bird appear right in front of my face? A bluetit! Then I would know that spirits are real!'

Whom was I talking to? Well, I wasn't sure, really. I'd already produced several books and published hundreds of articles on angels and the afterlife, and I guess I was talking to the spirits, the ghosts, call them what you will. I didn't mind which afterlife soul brought my sign. I'd have been happy with my loved ones doing it or a being of light complete with wings. Just someone nice, of course.

I write about the positive aspects of the paranormal every day. It's my job. I have seen so many things, yet after all this time even *I* feel the need for constant reassurance, for proof that I'm not tricking myself into believing some mystical mumbo jumbo. It's human nature, I guess. Is there an afterlife? Is there a heaven? I believe … but … just one more little sign?

Could I demand things? Could I ask them to bring me a specific sign like a particular bird appearing in a certain way?

A bluetit appearing in front of my eyes? Of course I could!

Three days later I was packing for a surprise trip away. It was my wedding anniversary and my husband and I were loading up our suitcases. I walked over to the mirror to collect some cosmetics that were sitting on the windowsill and I literally gasped with delight. A baby bluetit was fluttering at the window just a hand's length away. It was so close I felt that I could almost have reached out and touched it, and it hovered for several seconds right in front of my face before I burst out laughing. Well, that told me, didn't it? I'd asked for a sign, a bluetit specifically, and here it was! Once again I had my proof.

There is more to life than we see, hear and feel during normal waking consciousness – and I love it! Imagine never having to worry about death again because we know that when we pass over we are 'going home'. Imagine knowing that when we die our loved ones who have already passed over will be there waiting for us, like a big welcoming party. What if I could show you it was true? Do you want to believe? No? Well, read on, because you might have to think again.

Let's take a journey. A journey into the possibility that life might exist after physical death. Let's look at current research and real people's experiences, with a little bit of history thrown in for good measure. I'm not asking you to suspend belief, just to open yourself up to 'possibilities'. Is there anything else?

HOW DO WE KNOW THE AFTERLIFE IS REAL?

How do we know what happens when we die? Surprisingly, there is a lot of information available about what happens to the soul at the point of physical death and beyond. You don't have to 'die' to find out, although the 'near-death experience' – leaving the physical body at the point of death and seeing a white light at the end of a tunnel – can certainly give you a glimpse into what happens on the 'other side' of life. More of this later…

I have researched life, and the afterlife, for many, many years now. Like pieces of a puzzle, different pieces of information can be put together and we can begin to build up a picture of what happens when we die, where we go and what we do.

I may sound arrogant when I say this, but if a person doesn't believe in any sort of life after death, then I say to you that that person has not studied the evidence at all! There is just so much information out there and I felt it my duty – and an honour – to gather some of it here for you to review.

My sister Dilly told me once that she was approached by a man who said, 'All this stuff is a load of rubbish.' All *what* stuff? Had he investigated any of the material out there at all? I put it to you that *he* was very arrogant to dismiss it without any study at all.

Although I can't share everything I've ever learned, I want to walk you through the afterlife story in a way that will give the information you need to decide where (if anywhere) you want to go next with it. There may be times when you feel overwhelmed by it or that it really is just a load of rubbish. That's fine. You can dip into the book a little at a time or read it right though over the course of a few hours or days. Take your time if you need to, and if you feel inundated with material, put the book away, let the information sink in and come back to it when you're ready.

The information here is a 'snapshot' of my own learning. As with all authors, I interpret it in my own way and to you I say, 'Take what feels right to you right now and discard the rest.' Nevertheless, I hope that this book is one that you refer to over and over again as the years go by, and I hope most of all that it will take away your fear of death forever.

Death is something that concerns us all. Whether you have recently lost someone (or indeed *ever* lost someone in your life), or you have a close friend or relative who is dying right now, or you yourself are ill or have had a close call with death, or you work with the dying or the sick, I hope you find something here that will bring you a greater understanding of what is and what will be.

Let's have a little look.

CHAPTER 1

So, What Do We Know?

Reality is merely an illusion,
albeit a very persistent one.

ALBERT EINSTEIN

I believe that even though our physical bodies die, life continues on 'the other side'. There are many ways in which we catch a glimpse of the when, what and where of heaven, and these pieces all fit together like a giant jigsaw puzzle. Where do they come from?

• Personal stories of near-death experiences certainly give us more than a glimpse. We have cases of living human souls who have left their physical body at the point of death and returned because it was 'not their time' (people who've nearly drowned, had a non-fatal heart attack, etc). They often get to peek through the light at the end of the tunnel and can move temporarily to the 'other side'. On occasion they have been given the choice to stay on Earth or go to the light – go home to heaven. Sometimes the choice is made for them. Deceased friends and relatives may tell them to go back to live or even literally push them back into their body. More about this later! When they do come back, they bring tales of beautiful gardens full of flowers and trees, living bodies of water and colours which our human eyes cannot perceive, as well as amazing buildings full of the records of human life and places of learning for the soul. People have written similar accounts throughout history and today these stories are found all over the world. In case you're feeling sceptical, even young children report viewing heaven after a near-death experience and you just know that a two-year-old hasn't read on the Internet about what is supposed to happen!

- During bodily trauma (accidents and operations) the soul will sometimes leave the body and people often see deceased loved ones at this time.

- Children (and occasionally adults) spontaneously recall past lives and living in heaven before birth into this life. There have been many cases around the world, especially amongst pre-school children, where a child will recall a previous life and recall details of family members, the homes they lived in and the jobs that they did. Many of these fascinating memories have been checked out.

Imagine the fun when living relatives from the past life are still alive and are recognized by the young child. But this is a whole other area of research! Maybe you're now interested in researching past lives?

- During out-of-body experiences, the soul can fly free and meet loved ones who have previously crossed over, or it can temporarily visit heavenly realms. Out-of-body experiences can occur spontaneously, sometimes during bodily trauma (a little like a shorter version of the near-death experience). You can also make them happen using disciplined meditation techniques. I have tried and tested these myself (and many of the other things in this book).

- Mediums and psychics (those with the natural ability to communicate with the other side) sometimes bring information through about what it is like to be physically dead.

- Some people communicate with the other side using tools such as ouija boards (also called spirit boards or talking boards). Although there is much controversy surrounding such methods, many people do have great success with them. Like all of these things, there are negative stories and positive stories, but if you look closely enough, there is personal proof of the existence of the afterlife too. Much more about this later (and yes, I've tried this too).

- Another way we gain information about the afterlife is through hypnosis. Trained hypnotherapists around the world are now using deep hypnotic trance states to enable people to recall living in a heavenly realm before they were born and actually choosing their next life.

- What else? Ah yes, souls spontaneously visit their loved ones on Earth in dreams and visions. I have a great many stories to share on this very topic. Our loved ones often take the opportunity to explain what has happened to them and tell us about where they are living now. Does this sound unbelievable? Well, I'm convinced, so read on and decide for yourself!

- By studying the many thousands of real-life experiences of afterlife contact, near-death experience and so on, it is possible to build up a picture of what happens when we die, where we go and how we come back again. I have included some ideas for further research and some resources for you near the end of the book. The whole subject of life, the afterlife, past lives, new lives, afterlife contact, etc., is a vast one and sometimes it's difficult to know where to start – and end. But there are some dedicated people in the world who are currently working on proving these things for us. Don't let anyone tell you that there is no proof of life after death. There is plenty! How you interpret it is up to you. But in time you will start to create a picture of what else is out there and soon you too may be left in no doubt that there is more living to do once we leave this physical life. 'Death' as we know it is just the beginning.

******

There is a saying (well, several variations on a saying, actually): 'If it looks like a duck, sounds like a duck and acts like a duck, then in all likelihood it *is* a duck.' Consider this as you read on.

Not everyone has the time or the advantage that I have of being able to read thousands of personal accounts of afterlife contact or have access to the vast resource library that I have at my fingertips. So I'd like to assemble my findings for you here. I have gathered information from many different sources to share with you. The research is fascinating, and after many years, I have no doubts that life continues in some form, with conscious recall, after the death of the physical body. But how?

THE JOURNEY OF THE SOUL – WHAT HAPPENS WHEN WE DIE?

I would like to track for you the typical journey of a soul after leaving the body at physical death.

Before – when it's our time to go

When we say of someone, 'It was almost as if they knew they were going to die,' we're right. There is often an awareness that one is 'not long for this Earth' or that it's nearly time to go. This might happen after a long illness, because of the types of paranormal experiences the dying have or, on occasion, be a gut instinct which is almost a 'remembrance' of something we planned before birth.

One of my sisters works as a carer and one of her roles is helping out occasionally in a variety of retirement homes. One old gentleman told her quite confidently, 'I won't be here next week.' Actually he was, but his time was fairly close and as my sister only assisted at this home on an occasional basis he felt it unlikely that they would meet again. He was very happy about the whole thing, as he was in his nineties and was ready to 'go home' to heaven.

Announcing dreams

There is a phenomenon I call the 'announcing dream', where deceased relatives visit their living relatives in dream-like visions to warn them that it is time for them to go. There are some amazing examples of this later in the book.

Sometimes the dying actually see loved ones who have passed before. They have come to collect them and escort them 'home'. It is common to see deceased parents, partners and children in the days and weeks before we pass over as we slip in and out of consciousness. This is comforting to both the living and the dying.

If you know someone who has done this or is doing this, I have to point out here that this also happens during illnesses from which people do recover. Seeing the deceased does not necessarily mean you are going to die! More later.

'Deathbed visions'

For some people death can actually happen over a period of days or weeks. During this time it's as if they have 'a foot in both camps'. They can become very psychic and though it's easy for us to push aside 'deathbed ramblings' as pure nonsense, they may really be seeing Aunty Marge and Uncle Fred every morning! I truly believe that they are.

If you get the opportunity to talk to someone who is able to do this, you might be able to ask questions, depending on their state of consciousness at the time. You might be surprised at what you discover. Maybe you could receive proof of the afterlife as your loved one passes on to the next realm and brings you messages from the other side of life at the same time. Amazing!

Doctors, nurses and care workers tell me how common it is for the dying to suddenly gain the strength to sit up physically, even though they have previously been unconscious or too frail to do so. This is because they are seeing their loved ones in the other realms and want to reach out to them. They may even call out the names of those who have come to collect them.

Julie told me about her experience with her husband David (all the stories in this book have been shared with me personally, but personal details have been changed for confidentiality):

Going home to Mum

David was weak for the last two days before he died. He couldn't sit up, speak or anything really. He didn't eat or drink anything. It was clear that his time was close.

All of a sudden he pulled himself up – right up into a sitting position! I was amazed. He was staring at the corner of the room with a big smile on his face and I knew that he could see something amazing. He kept saying, 'Look, look...' Then he held out his arms and said one word, 'Mum!'

I was thrilled because I knew he was being collected and taken 'home'. He just looked so excited.

To watch someone who has been in such pain experience that – well, there's nothing like it in the world. It really helped my own pain because I knew that he was going to be OK in his new life in heaven.

On occasion people sitting with the dying are lucky enough to see the visitor as well as bear witness to the experience.

When the soul leaves the body other phenomena can be experienced too, both by the dying and by visitors in the room. There may be a strong smell of flowers or the sound of beautiful music playing. When large crowds of people are surrounding the dying, not everyone experiences these things, although there seems no logical reason why not. Some do and some don't, that's all.

Leaving the body

At the point of physical death the soul feels no pain. They say that hearing is the last sense to leave us, and this has been proved over and over again with the near-death experience. So if you sit with your loved one as they pass, remember that it's OK to say that you love them and send them on their way with blessings and special words. It's also likely that they will pick up your thoughts. Think nice thoughts!

It's common to be met on the journey home, as we've already seen with the previous story. Most people will see a loved one, a close friend, angels or a spiritual guide. Children are always collected. If we're not met it's because we are 'old hands' at taking the journey home – we've done it many times before and are happy to slip the short distance home alone.

When leaving the body many people feel light, free and euphoric, especially if they have previously been traumatized

It is important to mention here that if you are grieving following the loss of a loved one and are considering taking your own life, *DON'T*. Attempted suicides who come back from the brink almost always immediately regret trying to take their own life. By leaving prematurely, we've missed important lessons in our lives and just have to come back and do them again, and usually with a quick turnaround.

The American psychic Sylvia Browne, in her book *Life on the Other Side*, calls suicide 'a broken contract with God', although I feel there can be certain circumstances in which it is understandable, for example when it is our time to go and our life is simply being prolonged unnecessarily by medical technology. Being sad and missing someone, however, is not one of these circumstances. Remember the living whose lives you wreck by taking your own life. Sorry to sound harsh; just say I've been told a lot of stories of people who have gone through this (on both sides).

Spirits who come back to report from their side of life show concern for our grief and often work to prevent it. They seem to be able to tap into our lives a little ahead of time and know that we have more living to do and usually many loving years ahead of us. Life is for living and loving both ourselves and those around us, and this is one of the many reasons so many people around the world are receiving spontaneous afterlife communication. The 'dead' want us to carry on and even thrive after they pass (in time, of course).

or in great pain. We very quickly lose any attachment to the physical body. In the near-death experience, most people don't want to come back to this life, even when they have a choice. Strange, isn't it? We worry about dying and yet people who've 'been there' don't even want to come back.

WHAT'S IT LIKE ON THE OTHER SIDE?

Sonia's brother took her for a short visit:

Flying

My brother very sadly died of cancer and one day he came to me in the form of a dream. It was very special and magical. I commented on how well he looked and he reassured me that he was in great health. I asked him what it was like on the other side and he told me I could go with him and see for myself. I reminded him that he was dead and I wasn't, but he said that all I had to do was hold his hand and I could go with him. I wasn't frightened at all.

When I touched his hand it was very real, solid even, and it felt good to be so close to him again. Then the next thing I knew we appeared to be flying – not on an aeroplane or anything mechanical, just flying through the air – and it was an amazing feeling.

As I looked around me the things that struck me were the colours and the serenity of what was below us. The sense of peace was unbelievable and the fields looked beautiful. There appeared to be every shade of green you could think of and then probably more. I was talking to my brother about the colours when I realized we were standing in a garden. I commented on how beautiful it all looked and how lucky he was to be in such a wonderful place.

I noticed some daffodils and again the yellow wasn't like any other yellow I had ever seen. My brother said I could take some home with me, but I replied that I couldn't, as I didn't have any money. My brother laughed and said, 'You don't need money here. You can just take them.'

The next thing I knew I was back in my bedroom waking up from a dream and as I looked around the room, there on the chest of drawers were the daffodils. I jumped up because I was so excited and quickly got dressed so I could run down to my sister and tell her about the visit. To my surprise, when I got there she also had some daffodils.

At this point I really did wake up! I was so delighted and on such a high for some time afterwards because I know it hadn't been an ordinary dream.

Before he died my brother had said that if he could find a way he would let us know he was fine, and he fulfilled his promise. He came back to let me and my family know he was well.

This dream occurred nearly four years ago yet I still remember it as if it were yesterday.

WHAT DO WE DO THERE?

So what do we do in this wonderful place full of colour and serenity? There are many ways in which we can learn about this (*see Chapter 14: Is There a Heaven?*) Our lives on the other side are busy and fulfilled. Here are some of the things we do.

Review our past lives

We spend time reviewing our past life – the life we have just lived. We have the opportunity to look at all the moments that changed our lives in some way, both good and bad.

In their book *Lessons from the Light: What We Can Learn from the Near-Death Experience*, Kenneth Ring, PhD, and Evelyn Elsaesser Valarino relate the classic story of Neev, who explains that during his near-death experience he can see his whole life in front of him. Neev talks about all the good things and the bad that are shown to him, all the things that have occurred in his life up to the point of his physical death and the consequences of his actions upon his own life and those of others. He describes how he can literally feel the emotions of the people he has affected throughout his life. It's something we should consider carefully!

So, live a good life, die a good death ... and after death we learn about how we lived one life on Earth.

Meet our loved ones

It is clear that we meet up with deceased souls who are familiar to us from this life and also from other lives we have lived in the past. You'll remember them when you get there, I promise! We work with these 'soul groups' on many levels. Group members are attracted to each other by similar vibration. With these groups we continue to learn life skills. These can be pretty well anything, but include things like compassion, kindness, forgiveness, love and understanding, caring, any other positive human emotion and skill you can think of and more. So heaven is a kind of school too.

Live and learn with like-minded souls

It's a school with many classrooms; the realms of heaven are numerous. In the Bible (John 14:2) Jesus tells us, 'In my Father's house are many mansions; if it were not so, I would have told you. I go to prepare a place for you.'

When we die we go to the space which we have 'earned' through our soul development. We are literally attracted to the space that is correct for us. That is where our soul groups are, our soul families, the people with whom we share our earthly lives. So when we die, we go to live with others who are like us.

If you notice, this works in life too. In any country, similar souls group together. I'm not talking about monetary wealth or anything like that here, although rich and poor do tend to be together in different physical locations too, but about energy. There are always going to be places and people with whom we feel more comfortable and that's because we have a similar vibrational energy to them. Over time this can change, of course. When we start to feel unhappy in our jobs, for example, it's because we have outgrown our current position and it's time to move on. We change and grow throughout our lives and often change our friends so that we have friends who have similar interests to us. Heaven is like that too.

Unhappy people are people who are in the wrong place at the wrong time. To become happy again we need to take 'the next step up' – a slight stretch above where we feel we 'should' be.

In the realms of heaven, though, we are never going to find ourselves in the wrong dimension – we literally can't visit higher spaces until our souls are ready. So when we die, we end up in the right place and with like-minded souls who are at a similar soul development stage to our own.

What people have for many years called hell does not exist in the way we might think. But people whose lives have been spent on evil might well find themselves in the realms that the author George Richie called 'devoid of love' and the author Joy Snell called 'the sphere of ...wasted opportunities'.

We decide on our own place of 'rest', depending on our own review of our own lives, and are then attracted to that place. We are the ones who do the judging when we die.

There are no secrets – souls communicate through a thought process. Or, as one child put it, 'When I saw Granddad he spoke to me in my head. His mouth didn't move...' So who we are is apparent to all. If our thoughts and actions do not match, then everyone will know. Maybe it should be like this on Earth! We all know people who say nice things but we know that their thoughts are different.

Whatever our stage of development, there are lessons for us to learn. People have reported visiting 'classrooms' where they learn lessons related to their lives both in heaven and on Earth. Betty Eadie is one of them. She relates her near-death experiences in her book *Embraced by the Light.*

Other authors, including Raymond Moody and Melvin Morse, have described heavenly 'cities of light' or 'crystal realms'. These are just one area of heaven. In his book *Saved by the Light*, Dannion Brinkley shares the NDE experience in which he visited a crystal city and was escorted by a being of light.

A woman called Jacqueline once e-mailed to tell me about an experience when she 'nearly died' at the age of seven. She told me:

I can remember going to a strange world where buildings were transparent. Towards the end of my travels, I was being held in someone's arms and felt a lot of love. Then I was told it was not my time and I had to go back. At this I felt extremely upset. Then I remember waking up and feeling down for days.

As is typical of these experiences, Jacqueline was happier to be dead than alive!

Beautiful gardens are a regular feature of the heavenly realms. As we have seen, people who have visited them have described seeing flowers and plants in colours that our eyes cannot see on Earth.

There are also vast buildings that contain all knowledge. Everything that has ever been, everything that ever will be, all our history, all our lives, every thought and every deed of every person who has ever lived is recorded here. These buildings have been called 'the Halls of Knowledge', 'the Book of Life' and the 'Akashic Records'.

The 'sleeping prophet' Edgar Cayce (1877–1945) would drop into a trance state and apparently tap into the Akashic Records. He gave many thousands of psychic readings during his lifetime. A stenographer was present during the majority of them. The records of around 30,000 of these readings are currently held by the Association for Research and Enlightenment.

As it says in the Bible (Revelation 20:12):

I saw the dead, small and great, stand before God; and the books were opened; and another book was opened, which is the book of life: and the dead were judged out of these books, according to their works.

Also in the Bible (Psalm 139), David suggests that God has written down everything about him and all the details of his life both lived and yet to be lived. He says to God, 'In your book, all are written down...'

During his near-death experience Dannion Brinkley was shown what he called a 'cathedral of knowledge'. He was also shown several possible future scenarios for the world, which does indicate that not everything is laid down for us in advance. We do have choices about how to live our lives.

We've just touched the very edges of the afterlife realms here. Sadly, there is not room to go into any great detail in this, but I hope I have sparked an interest in further investigation. There are more ideas on this at the end of the book.

So let's move on, then.

VIBRATIONAL LIFE

We are vibrational people living in a vibrational universe. We are a moving mass of molecules and atoms – moving vibrational energy. We are not solid beings in the way we perceive ourselves to be. A solid wall is not really solid, a rock is not solid, this *solid* book is not actually solid at all – it is moving energy.

If you examine any object in our world closely enough you will see that nothing is as we perceive it with our human senses. Look though the right sort of microscope and you will see for yourself. We live in an illusion created by the way our brain translates our world.

So if you rely on your limited human senses, you are closing your mind to reality. Reality is *not* just what we *see*, *hear* and *feel* with our imperfect human senses. We know that the ultra-violet and infra-red ends of the light spectrum are outside our human range of vision, for example, but we know they exist because we can measure them. Imagine how many more colour vibrations must exist beyond those that we can currently measure. 'Physical reality' is just the tip of the iceberg!

Sound is another vibration. We know that different people can hear different ranges of sound and different pitches, and this can change as we age. We also know that some animals are able to hear sounds that are inaudible to the human ear, or sounds that we think are unlikely to reach them. My cats can hear me pouring their food into the bowls when they are out in my neighbours' gardens, even when I have the doors and windows closed in the house. Their sense of hearing amazes me, but it is natural to them. So even without scientific instruments we know that everything we hear isn't everything there is to hear!

Our sense of smell is also limited. Dogs, for example, can be trained to sniff out drugs and all sorts of other things. Their sense of smell is many times more powerful than our own.

Unfortunately, we often judge our whole world by what we receive through our very restricted human senses. How silly are we? We also make decisions about our lives by what we currently 'know' to be true. We base these assumptions upon our own personal experiences, other people's experiences (which can be useful), others' belief systems and the current scientific research into any given area. But it's important to remember that these things are changing constantly. What we believe today is absolutely and definitely *true* might change tomorrow when we have new technology that can measure and analyse things which are outside our current comprehension. Is the Earth flat? Of course not, and we know this now, but we didn't always. And scientists have discovered many more dimensions beyond the 3D world in which we exist!

Take this knowledge forward with you when you read the stories of afterlife contact that come later on in this book. Are most of us unable to experience our loved ones in the other realms simply because of the limitations of 'normal' human perception? Bear in mind that there have always been people who have had senses outside the normal range of human abilities. For many years they were persecuted and killed as witches, but many of these people *were* able to see people on the other side of life!

As you read on, do open up your mind to consider a wider reality.

CHAPTER 2

Ghosts or Spirits?

All I have seen teaches me to trust the
Creator for all I have not seen.
RALPH WALDO EMERSON

For many years people have been aware that spirits can contact the living using a medium or intermediary, someone with the ability to communicate between this world and the next. As we've said previously, there have always been people with this ability. We've considered them 'weird'. But what if they were just advanced souls'?

As a young girl I had plenty of 'weird' experiences of my own. I used to wake up regularly to see strange people-like shapes in my room, ghostly outlines. I was always frightened by them. No one really understood what I was seeing and we explained the experiences away as 'nightmares'. How I wish that I knew then what I know now. At the time I knew that my grandmother had frightening premonitions and later I discovered other family members who were well ahead of their time 'spiritually thinking' had experiences relating to psychic ability and healing skills. How I wish I'd had the opportunity to get to know these fascinating family members of earlier times – it would have made my own experiences easier to understand.

How many of us have had family members who could do these things but have never known about it? A great many, I feel.

HAUNTINGS AND SPIRIT VISITATIONS

There is a world of difference between a haunting and a spirit visitation. Ghosts haunt, while spirits visit. Ghosts can be many things: an 'energy memory' that has been recorded into the very fabric of a building (think of the way that voices are recorded on magnetic tape), lost souls who are hanging around familiar places on Earth, perhaps with unfinished business to attend to, and sometimes souls who don't know they are dead. Traumatic events and sudden deaths can temporarily trap a soul in a place and time, making them a ghost.

Ghosts are not usually known to the person who sees them. Some have consciousness and some do not. They can also be spirits who are visiting either a person or a place related to the earthly realms. They might be calling from another time and space, almost as a time traveller might. A haunting is when the spirit visitor appears over and over again … when they are not wanted.

A visit from a loved one is different from a ghost sighting in the same way that a knock on the door from a stranger is not the same a friend calling! The souls of our departed loved ones visit via a different link, attracted as a magnet to the love we once shared on Earth. Love creates a sort of satellite navigation system to help them find their way. Our loved ones don't just track us to our homes. They follow the link of our personality energy and can find us wherever we are in the world. Their visits are not hauntings but house calls. By the way, if your house caller is one you have not invited or don't want to see, then, as in real life, you can most certainly ask them to leave – and expect them to go too.

Thankfully, most spirit visitations are from those we love and who love us back. We never actually stop loving someone just because they have died in the physical world, and when they cross the divide between our realms and theirs, the one thing we notice before they arrive is that the love we shared is still right there between us.

There have always been stories of spontaneous afterlife contact, of loving relatives and friends reaching out from the other side to comfort and reassure people in times of need. But there have never been more of these stories than there are right now. Or maybe it just seems that way. Is it because of the Internet? Perhaps it's just that it's never been easier to find someone who shares our interests or will listen to our ramblings!

It's certainly true that there are chat rooms and Internet groups for just about everything nowadays. So if you've been lucky enough to have a spirit visitation from someone you love but unlucky enough to be unable to share it with your family and friends, you can guarantee that there is someone somewhere in the world who knows just how you feel because they've been there. If this is you, you can always e-mail me. I believe you.

In effect the Internet is a world-wide support system. We know we are no longer alone (and I'm not talking about extra-terrestrials of the *Alien* type) and it's easier to share experiences now than ever before. So perhaps this is why people are more willing to share their positive paranormal experiences?

It could also be that we are all becoming more spiritually aware. Are the veils between the worlds becoming thinner, as many have predicted? Are our loved ones becoming more adept at reaching those they have left behind on Earth? Who knows? All I can tell you is that I personally receive thousands of stories of spontaneous visitations from the afterlife from visitors to my website all over the world.

So, how do we open ourselves up for a visit? Being open to the possibility is a good way to start.

'See you soon!'

Debbie said goodnight to Frank and his wife Sarah as the two of them left the local bar late one Friday night. 'See you soon!' she yelled.

'I must spend more time chatting to Frank,' she thought as the couple walked out of the door.

Debbie and her husband Neil met friends regularly in their local and Debbie often spent time chatting with Sarah but rarely spoke to Frank, who talked mainly with the other men in the pub. Sarah and Frank were a friendly couple and although Debbie and Neil didn't know them very well, they did consider them to be mates. They fitted in well in the small village where they all lived.

After they had left, Neil mentioned that he'd been worried about Frank the evening before. 'I asked him if he was OK,' he said. 'He did say he felt a little unwell, but I'm sure he's OK now.'

But Frank, a family man in his early fifties, died of a heart attack the following evening. Debbie and Neil were shocked. Who would have guessed that feeling 'a little unwell' would have meant death the next day? It crossed Debbie's mind that she had never got to talk to Frank again after all, and she felt sad about it.

The following evening Debbie and Neil were busy packing their suitcases for a Christmas cruise. Debbie was particularly tired and went to bed early. No sooner had she fallen asleep than she started to dream that

Frank was standing there looking at her with a huge grin on his face. He looked happy and well.

Debbie was stunned. 'Why are you here?'

Frank apologized and explained that he'd tried everyone else but no one could see him but her. 'You left the door open,' he explained.

He wanted to let her know he was settling well into his new home. He showed her a particular brand of cigarettes and Debbie felt he was explaining that his smoking habit had caused his death. Even though she was actually unsure whether Frank had smoked or not, discreet enquiries the following day revealed that this had been his favourite brand.

Frank visited Debbie because he was able to get through to her. She had given him permission by saying 'See you soon!' Also, grief often closes the psychic doorway and as a casual friend she was saddened by his sudden death but not paralysed by it in the way that his family would be.

We want so badly to be able to see our loved ones after they die – we want to know that they continue to exist and are OK – but death is a traumatic event and the body will often go into shock. We disappear into a type of psychic bubble, letting nothing in and nothing out. We tighten control around our aura (natural energy field) and shut out feelings for fear of being hurt. Spontaneous contact from our loved ones relies on the 'love link', so they are shut out too. They might be sitting right next to us and we might not be able to feel anything at all. It's no one's fault.

In this situation a soul will often visit a young child, a neighbour or casual friend who will receive the visitation more easily. If this happens to you, it does leave you in a difficult situation, though. It's not easy to knock on someone's door and say, 'Sorry about your loss. By the way, I had a funny dream about your granddad last night!' In most cases it would be totally inappropriate to pass on a message which had not been sought. The people involved might suffer more and wonder, 'Why did he visit my neighbour and not me?' Not everyone would be ready for this sort of message, or even understand it; certainly not immediately following a death.

WHEN YOU WANT A VISIT FROM A LOVED ONE, WHY DON'T THEY COME?

Apart from grief, there are several other reasons why our loved ones can't come to us. Here are a few of them:

- If our loved ones didn't believe in life after death, they might not realize that they *can* visit us and might not try (although this isn't always a problem, so don't worry if you find yourself in this situation).

- If the death was sudden, they might not realize they are dead for a while.

- If the death followed a long illness or bodily trauma, the soul will be going through a period of healing first of all. Souls who need this often wake up in a hospital type of setting on the other side.

- If our loved one died by their own hand they will go through a type of healing process too and it might be some time before they can visit (but again, not always).

- Our loved ones can become so caught up in their new life that they are unaware of the passing of time. Time as we know it does not exist in heaven and this has been expressed many times in the visitation stories in my files.

- Souls are also busy learning about their new lives and are not always immediately aware of our yearning for them.

- Some souls might not be able to visit at first unless they are helped. Practice, though, makes perfect!

- Some might be able to get through, but we might not be able to receive their messages – through no fault of *our* own.

******

Not all souls find it difficult to visit us, though. Some get so good at it that they can stay for quite long periods or visit on a regular basis. They are very helpful in assisting contact with those who are experiencing difficulties with spirit communication. The following story explains it very well.

'It's not as easy as you think'

Before my granddad died I made him promise me that he would find a way to come and see me and let me know he'd arrived safely. He wasn't a believer, I have to say!

When he was in intensive care in hospital he said to me, 'I had a dream last night and if I ever get out of here I'll tell you about it.'

I couldn't wait for him to get out of hospital and after he'd recovered a bit and had some rest I asked him to tell me about the dream.

He said he was walking down a country lane and there were lots of people around him but they were all people that he knew were dead. They were all saying hello to him.

At the bottom of the lane he could see his mother and he was trying to get to her. But she shook her head and told him, 'It's not your time, go back.' [This is a classic phrase of the near-death experience.]

He died three weeks later, but I was always grateful that at least I had a chance to say goodbye to him. I didn't get any contact from him immediately after he died, though, and I felt angry with him because of the promise he'd made that he would show me he'd arrived OK.

The night he finally managed to get to me in a dream, he actually appeared out of breath. He said to me, 'At last I've got to you. It's not as easy as you think.'

That's all I can remember of that particular experience, but at least then I understood. I've had other dreams about him since, so I'm happy to say I think he's finally got the hang of it!

SIGNS

Our loved ones are ingenious in their attempts to prove they have continued to exist beyond physical death. They often use signs to let us know that their soul has lived on.

How can we recognize these signs? What is the difference between a sign and 'wishful thinking'? At a recent talk I gave to the grief counsellors at my local hospice I shared the following example. My mother (still living!) collects china cups and saucers. So cups and saucers are a symbol of our family's association with her and everything she represents in the way of a welcoming and comforting hostess. A cup of tea in a china cup and saucer is the way we celebrate family occasions and discuss family traumas. So if my mother were to bring a cup and saucer to me in some form after her own passing, I would immediately recognize it as a sign from her. To anyone else it would mean nothing at all, but to me it would mean everything.

Each family and each family member have their own signs. What objects do you associate with your own family members who have passed over? Use this as your starting point. Did your father go fishing? Was your brother's favourite object his motorbike? Did Grandma grow roses? Your family's symbols are your proof, no matter what anyone else's opinion might be!

Your sign might appear to you in a dream, as a physical gift from a friend or stranger, or as a picture in a magazine or advert on a billboard. Whatever it is, it will appear at a time when you need reassurance, maybe when you are grieving or distressed and often when you have actually asked for a sign. It will crop up in conversations or appear in a song on the radio. Maybe the song itself will be one of your signs!

Signs occur over and over again. They are 'synchronicities' which repeat on a regular basis and have a meaning for you (meaningful coincidences). A sign may also appear alongside a range of other phenomena.

Here is Michelle's story and one of her family signs.

A dragonfly

After Dad died we were told about a book to help children deal with bereavement. The book was about the life cycle of a dragonfly. That night my mam was out walking the dog and when she looked down, there at her feet was a dragonfly necklace shining away at her!

Coincidence? This is just one of many extraordinary events which surrounded Dad's passing!

Dragonflies often seem to act in unusual ways after a death and can become extraordinarily friendly and attentive! Birds do the same. Do loved ones arrive in the body of a bird, as some people believe? I think it's unlikely, but I do believe they have the ability to manipulate the energy of these creatures momentarily. Watch out for your own winged visitors.

In some cultures butterflies are seen as signs of spirit. They often appear around the time of a death (*see the extraordinary stories in Chapter 6: Do Animals Have a Soul?*) and alight on the coffin, sit alongside you in the funeral car or perch beside you at the graveside.

White feathers are also often seen as a sign of reassurance and comfort. Some people believe that they indicate a visit from their guardian angel. The grieving often find them appearing in unusual places and with perfect timing after they have requested a sign that their loved ones are still with them. A person might be sitting in a room alone with no feathers in sight, walk out momentarily, return and find a large white curly feather sitting squarely in the middle of the room! Could it be a present from a loved one? It just might be. I've written much more about this in my previous books.

OTHER FORMS OF CONTACT

A certain feeling

All over the world, the grieving 'feel' their loved ones around them. Each personality has a certain type of energy and we are very sensitive to this. We can often pick up on 'energy memories' too. When we walk into a room, for example, we can often feel if the people present have been rowing or shouting! Similarly, we might walk into a home and feel the cosy atmosphere that the occupants have left in the space.

When we first meet a person we gather impressions about them within seconds. Are they friendly or unfriendly? Happy or sad? Safe or unsafe? Much of this is done visually, but we also get a feeling about new people we meet – and we are usually right! Afterwards we might say 'I had a bad feeling about him' or 'I knew the minute I met you that we were going to be good friends…' Our intuition about the energy of another person is part of our natural survival skills.

We also remember the energy feeling that another person gives off and after death this feeling is the same. People often tell me that they 'felt' their loved one's energy draw close to them. You can't prove this to anyone else (not that you need to), but you just *know* they are there because you feel it in every part of your body. The air around you literally fizzes with energy, almost as if you have come into contact with an electrical current – which in a way you have.

Sometimes physical phenomena are associated with a visit from a loved one. You might feel the air around you go very cold (occasionally you feel warmer), or maybe your heartbeat quickens or you feel slightly dizzy. People usually report a sense of deep peace, calm and love. Our loved ones bring us that feeling that everything is going to be just fine.

A particular smell

It's not unusual for the recipient of a spirit visitation to smell something that they associate with the deceased. The smell of Granddad's tobacco, Dad's brand of cigarettes or the lavender hand cream favoured by Grandma might appear at the same moment as the visit. Strong floral scents are common.

You'd be amazed at the unusual scents that people share with me:

- Wet dog (Very nice!)

- Body odour (If any of my relatives are reading this, don't bother me with that one.)

- A *hospital* smell (disinfectants, medicines, etc.), which is often the last smell associated with the deceased

- 'The old cupboard at Grandma's'

- Fish and chips ('Granddad's favourite meal')

- Coconut ('Grandma used to bake cakes with this')

- Chocolate

- Motorbike oil.

...and the list goes on. If you can think of a smell, someone somewhere in the world has experienced it (and probably told me about it!). If your loved one thinks that you might recognize their signature scent, they might well try and reach you this way. I hope it's a nice one, for your sake.

Whispered words

Occasionally, words might be heard too. Yes, real words, in the voice of the person who has passed over. Usually the message is brief. It might include your name, their name or a short reassuring phrase like 'I'm OK now,' 'It's me' or 'I'm proud of you.' This seems to require an extraordinary effort on the spirits' part and this method of contact is most often reserved for emergency situations.

Personally, I've heard the words 'Test,' which woke me up one night, 'Pull over,' which saved me from a car accident, and 'Slow down' – another car accident avoided. I'm not sure that the word 'Test' achieved anything other than waking me up, come to think of it. I do remember that I woke up feeling very excited and I honestly thought, 'Great, they are going to be able to literally just chat in my ear now,' but it never happened like that again. Well, it hasn't happened yet, anyway.

It can be scary to hear the voice of a loved one from the other side, but remember it is done in love only. Ask for them not to contact you this way if you know you will be frightened. Which brings us to another question…

SHOULD WE BE FRIGHTENED?

Fear is a natural response to the unknown, and sensibly so in most cases. Being scared means the body is on high alert. We are super-sensitive and able to keep ourselves safe by taking action quickly. But this is different. Why be scared of someone you love?

Paranormal visual sightings at night often result in people hiding under the bedclothes or closing their eyes. When a visit is unexpected it might be a bit of a shock initially, but most people tell me that their loved ones bring such peace and love that the fear soon goes away. As you would imagine, second and third visits are less frightening than the first. Once you know what to expect, you are more prepared.

Most of the time we are visited by the spirits of those we loved and who loved us in return. On occasion, however, people do see the spirit energy of those who caused them mental or physical harm in life. In such cases the deceased is usually trying to make some sort of apology. This appears important for their spiritual growth as well as our own. Naturally it's up to you if you decide to accept it. Often, though, such visits won't be allowed and a relative of yours in the afterlife, a guide or angel or higher force will prevent the energy from coming to you.

If you do feel afraid at any time, you can always ask for spirit visits to stop. This almost always works, although in most cases people tell me they immediately regret asking their loved ones not to visit and spend years begging them to return! But it's important to know that you can take control.

DREAM VISITATIONS

Dream visitations are the least frightening of all visits and, as we have already seen, some of the easiest types of visit for the human brain to accept! Most things are easy to handle in a dream – pink flying elephants are normal when we are asleep. But anyone who has ever experienced a dream visitation will tell you that they are, in reality, *nothing* like an ordinary dream. The only similarity is that our body appears to be asleep. Our minds are most definitely not.

During the experience we interact with our loved ones as if they were standing right in front of us, which in a way they are. We almost always know they are dead and say so. You can read examples of this later. What is happening is that our loved ones are taking advantage of our minds being free and tapping into our dream experience.

On one particular night that this happened to me I found I was literally having an ordinary (boring) dream one minute and the next it was as if someone had changed the channel on the TV and a real-life person was walking right out of the screen to interact with me. That person was a 'real-life' loved one, someone I had known in life, and, as in all classic visitation dreams, I *knew* that he was dead!

VISIONS

Although in waking life seeing the spirits of our loved ones is normally something only a medium is able to do, on rare occasions 'ordinary' people do see them. This is probably more due to what the spirits are doing than to some miraculous new abilities of our own, unfortunately.

In my experience certain conditions make this more likely:

- When we are on the edge of sleep – either just waking or just about to fall asleep. Spirits can wake us up too.

- When we are meditating

- When we are tired (and our consciousness is altered slightly from the normal)

- When we are driving (again it's due to that altered state of consciousness that comes when we are doing something repetitive or which comes 'naturally' to us and allows us to daydream). They don't do this unless it's urgent, though – naturally the shock of seeing a dead person next to you might cause a few problems of its own.

- When we are daydreaming during boring chores (ironing, washing up, washing down tables and so on), or just bored in general. Random wandering of the mind can open up the senses to psychic phenomena and so we might hear, smell or feel something then too.

- When we are unconscious (for example during an operation or illness)

- During bodily trauma.

******

Sometimes the visual sighting of a loved one can occur for no apparent reason at all – maybe it's just because *they* can do it then.

PHYSICAL PHENOMENA

I just want to quickly share with you some of the other things that spirits can do. Their actions are quite clever, really. They use all sorts of tricks to get your attention. They can turn on your water taps and mess about with the electricity of the house, making lights flicker, for example, or turning on things which are not even plugged in. In fact, I remember an early experience with this. We had a portable television and one day it switched itself on. I double-checked that it wasn't plugged in – it wasn't – and then asked my mother to come and check. I even wondered if it might have had an internal battery of some sort, but it didn't. Someone was trying to get my attention!

Your loved ones can also mess about with candles and flames, making patterns of them; arrange for your favourite song to play when you walk into a shop or their favourite song to play when you ask for a sign; set off alarm clocks and other alarms; mess with clockwork toys and music boxes and so on.

New technology is a favourite. They love computers and mobile telephones and use them to get messages to us as often as they can. Dead? No way. What dead person would be able to do these sorts of things?!

'Coincidences'

Coincidences? I don't believe in them. Spirits love to arrange for us to be at a certain place at a certain time so that we pick up a message. It's not a coincidence at all if we suddenly bump into someone who can help us or see or hear something that will comfort us.

Lots of the stories people send me include this type of phenomenon and I've had some strange experiences of my own too. You'll find some of the stories later in this book.

If you feel you need a bit of support or reassurance, ask your loved ones for help. Then watch for the signs. Be ready for 'coincidences' to start happening in your life.

CHAPTER 3

Why Do They Visit?

Where there is love there is life.
MAHATMA GANDHI

Why do the dead visit the living? Actually for all of the reasons you might expect.

TO REASSURE US THEY'RE OK

For the most part, our loved ones on the other side want to reassure us that they are alive and well, simply in another place. Once they leave their physical bodies they realize that they haven't ceased to exist at all – quite the opposite, in fact – and they want to let us know that they're fine.

Many people report that the deceased appear to be in 'complete elation and ecstasy' at finding themselves in their new home – the realms they call 'our real place of existence'. Although they seem very much aware of our powerful feelings of loss, because they have now gained a wider knowledge of how life and physical death 'work' they don't suffer the loss of the physical relationship in the same way that we do. They miss us, but know that this isn't the end.

Although 'deceased', they appear well and usually show themselves to us as they were in the prime of life, often looking years younger than when they died. Children who have crossed over sometimes show themselves as young adults, or they can appear to have grown up in accordance with the passing years here.

Young children are more likely to see relatives in such a way that they will recognize them, but they nearly always appear fit and healthy.

Megan initially wrote to tell me about her own experiences and then forwarded an e-mail her sister had sent her about her niece, nine-year-old Ashton, who was visited by her recently deceased grandfather:

Whole again

Ashton got visited last night! She woke up and was so excited to tell me that Grandpa had visited. I asked her what she was talking about and she explained that in her dreams she got to see Grandpa. I asked her to tell me her dream and had her write it down so she wouldn't forget it.

She said that in the dream she was walking into the school cafeteria when she saw a group of old people there and then all of a sudden she saw her grandpa stand up and could hear him laughing and talking. He appeared to be playing cards with her other grandpa and grandma. She said the man had a round bald head and some grey hair by his ears like Grandpa Woodrow and the lady had really grey hair and had flowers on her shirt. That sounded like Grandma Fay to me!

I asked her when Grandpa Bill stood up if he had both of his legs and Ashton said yes. He stood very tall and didn't even walk with a limp. She told me that he didn't have his crutches or walker, although he was wearing his glasses.

The dream was so vivid for her and she was so excited by it. She told me that Grandpa would come see me too if I just talked to God and asked him how Grandpa was doing and told him that I really wanted to see him again. I tell you, there is something about the mind of a child that is so open that I think her own prayers were definitely answered. She was really happy to know that Dad was not in pain and the smile on his face was very reassuring to her. I think Grandpa showed Ashton that he was no longer ill but kept on his glasses so that she was able to recognize him.

I had a similar experience myself when a family friend appeared to me after she had passed. In the dream she showed herself to me with black hair and it wasn't until I woke up that I remembered that she used to look that way. When I was a child she had always coloured her hair a very dark shade, but when I had seen her last she had had silvery-grey hair! However, she showed herself to me in a way that she felt was her 'best'.

TO PASS ON MESSAGES

Our loved ones bring the same sorts of messages through over and over again. Here are some of the most common ones:

'I love you.'

'I'm still with you. I haven't left you.'

'I want you to know that I'm OK now.'

'I'm keeping a promise I made with you before I died and showing you I've arrived safely.'

'Stop worrying about me.'

'Carry on with your life.'

'I'm proud of you.'

'I'm aware of your achievements.'

'I've met up with Mum/Dad/my brother/etc.'

'I'm worried about *you* because you are still grieving for me.'

'It's beautiful in the place where I am now.'

'I'm here to say goodbye.'

'You're going to be all right.'

******

On occasion they also bring us information that we were previously unaware of. This both acts as proof that the experience is real and also helps us in our day-to-day life without them. Here is an example of the 'something you find out about later' type of story.

White lining

Paula told me that when her grandma was alive she was interfering, opinionated and demanding – but she still loved her with all her heart.

After she died Paula often dreamed about her, but said that she put the dreams down to 'wishful thinking' rather than accepting the possibility that they might include real visits.

After one particular dream Paula woke her husband, who encouraged her to call her brother, as parts of the dream involved him and his family. The dream had seemed so real that Paula did share it with her brother. He made her promise not to discuss it with anyone else and Paula readily agreed.

Several months later, Paula's mother called her. She said, 'Your brother says I've got to phone you straight away and say to you: "White lining!"'

Paula didn't hear her properly and was confused. 'What are you on about? Why does Andrew want you to talk to me about white lightning? Does he want me to buy him some of the drink?'

Her mother laughed and explained, 'Not white lightning, white lining...'

At this point Paula went cold all over and said goodbye to her mother as quickly as she could. Then she immediately phoned her brother. She explained:

My dream had been about my grandma. In my dream, she had said that she was still watching over all of us and to prove this she knew that my brother had just become a proud dad to Frederick and said she was now watching over him as well. To further prove her point, she said that my mum would send the baby a new hat in the post. It was going to be similar to a deer-stalker in style and would be brown with a furry white lining. Guess what my brother had received that morning?

What a fun story and it perfectly demonstrates this type of dream visitation experience!

TO OFFER SUPPORT

We all have problems in our lives. It's part of being alive! We don't expect even our closest friends to sort out our problems for us, but what is important is to know that they are supportive and they care about us.

This is what our loved ones want to do for us once they pass to spirit. I see this in messages from loved ones over and over again. They want to let us know that they are there for us. They can't always change things for us, although you know they often can (I'll get to that in a minute), but they are aware of what is happening to us and still care.

A story sent to me by a lady called Jean illustrates this point.

'It's all right'

Mum died four months after a massive stroke and she never regained her speech. After this we had other tragedies in the family which made life very stressful. A few months after my mother's death, my son's marriage broke up and he was devastated. I really felt his pain with him, as mums do. We were just starting to come to terms with that when my daughter came to us distraught, telling us that her husband had told her he didn't love her any more and was leaving her and their two little girls.

I had to be strong for them, but when I was on my own I just fell apart. I don't think I've ever felt quite as low as I did then and I couldn't see any silver lining.

One morning I was lying in bed just after my husband had left for his early shift at work. I was staring at the ceiling and then I drifted off to sleep very suddenly. I found myself in a very misty grey room, sitting with what seemed like an old-fashioned wooden shop counter in front of me. Then my mum was there, sitting on the other side, and she took my hands in hers and said, 'It's all right, it's all right.' And you know what, I could feel her holding my hands and I knew if I opened my eyes she would be gone, so I tried hard not to, but I had to.

Actually, I have never been able to sleep on my back, so I don't think I was sleeping at all. But the 'dream' had such an effect on me that I was very emotional all day and it is still as clear to me now, ten years later.

It's amazing how these dream visitations stay with people for years and years and remain clear in the mind. You don't easily forget a visit from a loved one from another realm of existence! With Jean, it's not likely that her mother could do anything other than bring comfort, but just then comfort was perfect.

TO HELP US

OK, so I promised you that I would share with you some of the ways in which our loved ones actually help us on this side of existence. First of all, let me tell you that sometimes they help us when they are not supposed to – but more of that in a minute!

One way is by bringing people into our lives to help us. So watch out for 'coincidental' encounters, especially if you have asked for help.

Another way is by sending us love. That energy fills us, topping us up in a healing way. In fact with some visits, the spirit is not seen or heard but felt, and this loving feeling is often exactly what we need at that moment.

On occasion our loved ones can also reach through the veil and warn us that our lives are in danger. I have numerous stories of this type of phenomenon. As long as the danger is not something we planned to have in our lives as a 'life lesson', spirits will be able to help. One day when driving along in my car I heard a voice tell me to pull over to the side of the road and in doing so I narrowly missed a head-on collision with a van which was coming in the opposite direction in the middle of the road. The van actually clipped my wing mirror, but I was completely safe. So the voice saved me from a serious accident.

I received a letter from a lady who heard a familiar voice give her a warning when she was driving her car one day. Later he came to her in a dream and called himself her 'driving angel'.

As I mentioned earlier, it's hard for spirits to bring a voice vibration through to us, so their messages are usually brief, but they can say 'Slow down,' 'Pull over,' 'Go a different route' or whatever. If you hear the voice of a loved one bringing you a message of this sort you will know that it's hard to resist the pull! People tell me, 'I *had* to listen.' Spirits know this and so they save this voice vibration for emergencies.

Now there is a weird 'postscript' to this observation. Allow me to explain. Whilst I was writing this section of the chapter my daughter came in and asked me the time. It was 4 p.m., so I remember the exact time I was writing this out.

Move forward five hours. I telephoned my sister Debbie to ask her if she was interested in buying my car. She wasn't, but we got chatting and talked for around 15 minutes, covering many subjects, as you do! Just as I was about to say goodbye, she said to me, 'Oh, I forgot, John's dad came to me today and gave me a message...' This caught my attention, as John is my husband and so we were talking about my deceased father-in-law!

Debbie went on to explain. Apparently at the exact time I was writing this section of the book, unbeknown to her, she was driving into town with my niece. As she did so, she heard the voice of my late father-in-law telling her to take a different route. She said that in her mind's eye she could see a large lorry, so decided right away to take the back roads into town. Then my father-in-law said, 'Tell Jacky I helped you.'

Now of course my sister had no idea why he would have said this, but we know now, don't we? Very conveniently, he was giving me a brilliant example to include in the book. My sister was stunned when I explained. She'd been used as a (very willing) pawn in the whole operation! Thanks, Father-in-law!

Experienced drivers work on 'autopilot'. What I mean is that a lot of our driving skills are unconscious. We might drive for many miles and be deep in thought and not really remember much of the journey. This 'daydreaming' state is ideal for connecting to the other side – as well as for picking up divine inspiration! Debbie has picked up messages from 'the other side' when she has been driving before. It seems that this form of communication is particularly good for her. Maybe it will be for you too!

Now back to my previous comment. When I say that *sometimes* our loved ones help us when really they shouldn't, it's because they are involved in our lives in the same way that they would be if they were still alive on Earth. Usually we are helped from the unseen realms by spirit guides. These are advanced souls who have almost always lived at least one human life. They have the advantage of being able to access our chosen life path and their role is to help guide us through the lessons we chose to experience before birth. Part of what they do is to step back and let us make mistakes. Making mistakes can be a great way to learn.

Let's put it like this: your baby is learning to walk and you watch them fall over. Do you a) reach out and hold their hand so that they can walk with your help or b) encourage them but let them learn to walk on their own by trying different things, some of which will involve them falling over again and again? Does that make sense? Of course we want our children to be able to walk unaided if it is possible for them to do. We can't be following them around into adulthood, just in case they trip. And if we let them, they will learn.

We can also use this as a metaphor for life. Sometimes it's more useful to have a *little* input than a lot, so that we can learn a task or skill for ourselves. We are here to learn, after all. And what would we learn if someone else did everything for us? Why bother coming to Earth at all?

Our families and friends (living and dead) aren't so good at standing back, though. Because they love us (remember that death doesn't change that) and hate to see us get hurt, they can sometimes jump in enthusiastically in an effort to help us. I've literally had dream visitations where loved ones have started to tell me something but then been cut off by a higher source, because the lesson ahead is something that we on Earth have to learn for ourselves.

Remember this when you are grieving and struggling with life problems. Feel your loved ones around you and know that they are supporting you, but that ultimately, as with all things in life, we have to work things out for ourselves – OK, possibly with a little bit of help! The hand of friendship is always welcome – from either side of life.

TO LOOK AFTER US WHEN WE ARE UNWELL

It is common for a spirit visitation to take place when a family member is unwell, unconscious or in hospital. Our loved ones appear to comfort, protect and bring healing. Here is Danielle's story:

'Great Granddad watches over me'

In April of 2005 I was taken into hospital with a severe chest infection and it caused my lungs to deteriorate. I was sent to the intensive care unit, where I was put on life support and was even given a tracheotomy to help my breathing.

I was unconscious for a week and when I eventually woke, I felt as though I didn't want to go back to sleep ever again. I was simply terrified to close my eyes in case I never woke again. I stayed awake for three whole days and the nurses even gave me sleeping tablets to try to help me, but they didn't seem to work. I was just too anxious.

On the third night I still hadn't slept I was getting desperate. My mum went home and I tried again, but I could only close my eyes for a couple of seconds before they bounced open again.

Then something different happened. As I closed my eyes I saw the face of my great grandfather. He was just above my face and he smiled at me and told me that it was OK. I was stunned, but I knew then that I wasn't alone. A large tear rolled down my cheek and I closed my eyes and drifted right off to sleep.

When I woke the next morning, my mum was already there. I explained what had happened the night before and she believed my great grandfather had been with me the whole time. I felt so much more relaxed knowing that he was watching over me and I hold him responsible for my speedy recovery.

SO WHAT CAN'T THEY DO?

What I should say is 'What *shouldn't* they do?' because there are always rule-breakers! But that means there are rules too...

- They can't give you the winning lottery numbers. Sometimes they do help out with money, though. 'Unexpected' cash can arrive if you are desperate. Human helpers can finance things out of the blue and I do believe that our loved ones on this side of life can be influenced by those on the other side. OK, I'll admit it, I *have* known people to have dream visitations where they were told, 'Go and buy a lottery ticket today,' and they won. When I asked for the numbers myself, though, I was told, 'Stand on your own two feet!' Thanks a lot, guys.

- They can't give you too much information about what is coming up in your life. ('Will I get married again?' and that sort of thing.) However, if you have a court case coming up and the outcome is positive, they might well share that sort of information with you. Again, people have sent me stories about this. Although our loved ones *shouldn't* let us know about this stuff, sometimes they can't help themselves – and we're always grateful, of course.

- They can't solve all your life problems. Perhaps your biggest lesson in this life actually *is* to stand on your own two feet. Maybe it's important for your soul growth that you *do* work things out for yourself. But your loved ones still can help.

- They can't save your life if it is your time – usually! (There's that word 'usually' again!) And if you do something stupid like walk into the path of an oncoming car to test them and see if they are with you, be prepared to suffer the consequences of your actions. We do have to take responsibility for our own lives.

- They can't give you the answers to your exam questions, but might sit with you whilst you study or help you to find someone who can tutor you.

- They can't make you slim, fit or attractive. That comes from within you as a person. But you can ask them to help you 'coincidentally' bump into people who could help you to lose weight or build your confidence.

- They can't make a particular person love you – that goes against free will – but they might help you look for a person who can love you.

- They can't act as your guardian angels. OK, they might do so from time to time, but that is not their role as such. We do have our own guardian angels and spiritual guides as well.

******

Remember that your deceased loved ones are not there to do your every bidding. They are not your spiritual slaves or soul servants. They want to help you to move on in your life, but they do have their own lives to live in their new homes. Just know that they are around when they can be. They feel your pain, hear you when you talk about them and love you still. I've had stacks of stories to back up all of these statements.

SO WHAT ELSE *CAN* THEY DO?

Our deceased friends and families seem to keep up-to-date with what is happening in our lives and be aware of all the major milestones. Many spirit visits follow a family birth or wedding. Our loved ones often like to tell us that they were sitting in the audience as we received our awards, or that they are aware we have passed our driving test, and so on. They are proud of us and want us to know. Yes, this means *you*.

Barbara shares her touching story.

Shaking hands

My wonderful father passed away from a dreadful and rare type of motor neurone disease with a frontal lobe dementia. He had never a day's illness in his life and then he became ill at 55! It was an awful time for us. We were so close. I was Daddy's girl. He lost the ability to talk and swallowing was very difficult. He couldn't communicate properly during the last nine months or so. Eventually, in hospital, he passed away peacefully in his sleep. I was with him and held his hand as he died.

Yet Dad has never left completely. I often smell his aftershave. It appears regularly when I am sitting in the car on my own. No one else in the family uses the same scent that he did. I sometimes smell beautiful fresh flowers too, when there aren't any around. I know he is with me and I do talk to him often. I sense his presence.

My most amazing experience was a dream visitation from Dad. I was going through a tough time with my mum, who is elderly and quite frail. In the dream I asked my dad for his help, as I wasn't coping well and felt stressed over the whole situation. In the dream he was on the other side of the road and crossed over to see me. He put his arms round me and held me while I cried and told him what a terrible time I was having. It was so wonderful to feel my dad's arms around me and I knew that from then on he would always watch over me and help whenever he could.

Then later, in another dream, I was on the phone chatting to my mum when I happened to look through the back window and saw my dad walking past. I told Mum I'd have to go as I had just seen Dad and ran to the back door just as he was walking down the front drive. I called to him and he turned and came towards me and into the house. He'd never visited this house when he was on Earth and I'd always felt sad that he'd never had the opportunity to meet my second husband, but in the dream I actually introduced them to each other and they shook hands. How amazing is that?

He didn't stay long and I was disappointed when he said he had to leave. I watched him walk down the driveway and he turned and waved. It was truly a wonderful experience and so vivid.

Since then I have dreamed of him often. Usually he's in a room with lots of the family, both those still on Earth and those who have passed. In the dreams I am aware he has passed, but he always looks well and can talk. I am always aware how wonderful it is that he is talking. I now know he is OK in his new spiritual body.

Notice in this experience how Barbara's dad shows symbolically that he is on the 'other side' by standing on the other side of the road and that he momentarily 'crosses over' for a visit. Spirits love symbolism and you will notice other symbols in the experiences that appear throughout the book.

On occasion our loved ones can gather living and deceased relatives together during dream visitations, as Barbara's dad did here. Sometimes other earthly relatives will remember the dream visitation as well, so it's certainly worth asking them about it!

Our relatives love to pop in and visit the new babies in the family too, as this story illustrates:

An angel watching over me

My father-in-law was a kind and caring man who suffered most of his life with illness and sadly he passed away when I was five months pregnant with our first child. Padraig was born on 20 September 2001. My husband was very happy, but at the same time sad that his father would never see our beautiful son. I told him that his father could see him, though, because I have always believed that there is an afterlife.

When Padraig was four we had our proof. One morning he told me that his granddad in heaven had come down to see him and told him that he was always watching over him and loved him very much. We were thrilled. I asked my son to describe him, which he did very well, and he also said that he tried to touch his granddad but his hand went right through him! He added that his granddad had told him he could not show himself to my husband as he was too sad and it might frighten him.

Since then my son and now my daughter have talked about their grandfather often. As I walked past my daughter's bedroom the other day she was waving goodbye up to the ceiling and when I asked who she was waving to, she said her granddad of course.

I am glad that they have a wonderful angel watching over them.

It's very comforting to know that our loved ones are watching over us – our personal guardian angels. It's also interesting to note here that there was a problem with this gentleman's spirit manifesting to his son. Our loved ones in spirit always try to act in our best interests and are wary of making our grief worse than it is already. They can find it difficult to visit when it might not be appropriate.

Here is another experience from Jean, whose story of her mother visiting to comfort her appears earlier in this chapter. In this story, her father pops in to see a new member of the family and then symbolically indicates the distance he has travelled and the challenge of creating a dream visitation experience.

Checking on the baby

When my son was born 42 years ago, I had a vivid dream of my dad, who had died four years earlier.

In the dream someone knocked on my door and when I answered I found my dad outside. I was so pleased to see him and asked him if he wanted to come in. 'Everyone's here,' I told him.

Dad said, 'No. I have just come to see if the baby is all right and now I have a long way to go.' He indicated a lovely shiny coach parked on the road. He was a bus driver all his working life.

I have never forgotten that dream … it meant such a lot to me.

CHAPTER 4

Reaching Out

Unable are the Loved to die ...
for Love is Immortality.

EMILY DICKINSON

Traditionally, spirits have communicated with the living through mediums and psychics and the use of a wide range of psychic phenomena. Some of these methods are outlined in this chapter. Many people believe, as do I, that they shouldn't be attempted without due caution and using 'psychic protection' (including prayer and energy clearing of the space and the people involved). In other words, don't dabble. Don't mess with things you don't understand! Don't go searching for trouble...

Whereas the spirits of our relatives and friends come in love, by conducting a psychic sitting (séance) you can leave yourself open to other phenomena and unwittingly encourage negative and troublesome spirits. I'm not saying 'Don't go out and learn if you feel you want to,' but, like driving a car, spirit communication using the methods in this chapter requires some knowledge and experience before taking to the wheel! It's easy to tap into something you don't want to. And you don't have to believe in spirits to experience the paranormal phenomena which can be involved in making contact with the other side!

OK, now I've given you a dire warning, I have to say I've done most of the things here and never come to any harm whatsoever, but you expected a warning, didn't you? So don't ring me up if you mess with this stuff and have a problem!

THE FOX SISTERS – THE BIRTH OF SPIRITUALISM

'Can you copy the sound of these clicks?' asked Kate of the invisible noise-maker in her home. She snapped her fingers and the spirit immediately responded by echoing the sound exactly with knocks and raps. The annoying knocking which had plagued the family for weeks appeared to have intelligence behind it! Something unseen was 'talking' to them.

Kate Fox and her sister Margaret were living near Rochester, New York, with their parents. It was 31 March 1848 and the house already had a reputation for being haunted, but now it was becoming clear that the 'ghost' was able to interact with the family. The events drew much interest and even the neighbours were called in to witness the spectacle. During the next few days a code was developed and the family managed to establish that the knocker was the spirit of a gentleman called Charles B. Rosma, who was, he said, a murdered peddler who'd been buried in the cellar. No missing person of this name was ever traced, but locals helped dig in the cellar and a few bones were actually found. Bizarrely, many years later, in 1904, a skeleton was found walled up in the cellar!

During the commotion the Fox sisters were sent away to stay with other family members, but the knockings and rappings followed them. Soon word of the girls' talents spread and people travelled from far and wide to have 'readings' with the young 'mediums'. Everyone wanted to talk with the dead.

Kate in particular was able to produce a range of phenomena, including floating lights and hands. She was also able to communicate using spirit writing and was instrumental in moving objects from a distance. She was examined by the scientist William Crookes, who tested her in every way he could think of. He later said that he felt her abilities were genuine and not produced by trickery or fraud.

The religion of Spiritualism grew up around the sisters' ability to communicate with spirits and later many other mediums appeared around the world. Maybe up until this point they had chosen not to admit to their skills for fear of ridicule. As already mentioned, people with such abilities had once been burned as 'witches'.

Over the years there was always a question of how the Fox sisters had produced the phenomena, particularly the knocking and rapping sounds. They were accused of cracking their toe joints to make the sounds (at one point, Margaret herself demonstrated this ability in a theatre with doctors present to confirm that she *was* making the sounds), although people who had sat in sessions with them and experienced the knocking sounds on ceilings, walls, floors and even their own bodies were never impressed by this theory! Perhaps Margaret was trying to throw the scientists off track?

During Victorian times Spiritualism became very popular. Mediumship was big business and attracted lots of fraudsters as well as genuine mediums. Physical mediumship (*see below*) was much in abundance at that time. The Victorians needed to see their spirits, but unfortunately this offered the fraudsters the perfect opportunity. Working with hidden assistants in the near darkness of the séance room, they would make objects fly around and lights flicker off and on – yet often these things genuinely happened for real too! 'Table tipping' and 'spirit boards' were also used at this time.

Later, during the First and Second World Wars, grieving young widows often gathered together to explore afterlife contact. People were desperate to make contact with their sons, brothers and husbands lost in the war. In many of these sessions money didn't even change hands and séances were performed in private households. Dedicated and genuine mediums would often keep lengthy records of their get-togethers, recording messages from unknown soldiers who were purported to have died in the war.

Let's take a closer look at mediumship.

MEDIUMSHIP

The role of a medium is to act as an intermediary between the souls of heaven and Earth. All mediums are psychic (able to gain information through abilities outside the normal senses) but not all psychics are mediums (able to connect to spirits).

Mediums make contact with the other side in a variety of ways, including one or more of the following:

- Clairvoyance (clear sight): The ability to pick up visual information from the other side. This might mean using the physical eyes but is more likely to mean using 'clairvoyant vision', which is the ability to see information with the 'inner eye' – as if you were simply seeing the images in your mind. It's a little like when you use your imagination or visualize things in your mind.

- Clairaudience (clear hearing): Again this could be using the physical ears, but it's more likely that the voice will be 'heard' within the mind. Even though this information comes 'to mind' it doesn't mean that the medium hears a separate and distinct voice from their own. Usually it's the *interpretation* of what they hear, which is often information that comes to them out of the blue and was unknown to them before.

- Clairsentience (gut instinct/clear feeling or sensing): Many people who wouldn't consider themselves to be mediums might get a sense of a spirit visitor through clairsentience. It's difficult to define, but is a certain 'knowing'.

- Clairgustance/clairhambience (clear tasting): The ability to taste spirit presence is much rarer. It might simply involve the spirit passing on flavours of food they enjoyed during life. This is not as strange as it might at first seem. If Granddad loved coconut cake and a medium were to pick up the strong taste of coconut, it could be a great way of bringing you the confirmation that you need!

- Clairalience/clairfragrance (clear smelling): This is the ability to pick up psychic information using smell. It's not always as nasty as it sounds! (A less sophisticated person might go 'Ha, ha!' here.) As already mentioned, many spirits announce their arrival by the scent of flowers, perfume or their favourite tobacco – as well as other things!

- Claircognizance (instinct/intuition/clear knowing): The mother of a very young medium once told me that her daughter often picked up information in this way.

When questioned as to where the information came from, the young girl would say, 'I just *knowed* it in my head!' I couldn't put it better myself!

******

Over the years there have been many famous and powerful mediums. Helen Duncan was particularly special and deserves a mention here.

Helen Duncan, the proven psychic

Scottish housewife Helen Duncan, the mother of six children, brought hope to thousands during her lifetime – 1897–1956 – and played an important role in proving life after death. She found herself in the middle of controversy during World War II. During a séance she brought forth the image of a dead sailor with the name HMS *Barham* on his cap. The sailor announced to the medium that he had died when his ship had been sunk. The government of the day denied the very existence of the ship and its loss was not officially announced until three months later. How else could Helen have known such information if not through her mediumship? Nevertheless, she ended up in court, charged under the ancient 1735 Witchcraft Act, which also covered fraudulent spiritual activity.

Helen had proved herself a genuine medium many times over the years and some of her clients came to court to act in her defence. The author Alfred Dodd shared his own experiences with the court. He explained how his own grandfather had 'materialized' during a séance led by Helen. He said his grandfather was fully dressed and talking during the encounter.

During another sitting attended by a gentleman called Vincent Woodcock (who also testified on Helen's behalf) and his sister-in-law, Helen had produced ectoplasm to manifest Vincent's dead wife. Ectoplasm often appeared in séances in the past. It was a cloudy type of matter that seemed to seep out of the body of a medium during trance. Spirits were apparently able to manipulate it into their own form to make themselves visible and audible. It was thought that to disturb a medium in this trance state could endanger their life.

At Helen's séance the spirit form of Vincent's wife spoke and asked both Vincent and his sister-in-law to stand up. The deceased then proceeded to remove her wedding band and place it on her sister's wedding finger, at the same time announcing her wish that the two of them be married for the sake of her little girl. They were indeed married a year later and returned to Helen for a further visit, in which the spirit form again appeared, this time to offer her congratulations on the nuptials.

Helen had given hundreds of readings in Spiritualist churches up and down the country in which she had brought forward spirits in a physical form who were able to talk and even touch their grieving relatives in this way.

Nevertheless, she was found guilty in court, and not because she wasn't a genuine medium – quite the contrary. The government was worried that through her mediumship she would inadvertently leak classified wartime secrets.

Helen was sent to Holloway prison for nine months. Many believed it was a serious miscarriage of justice and the prison warders agreed. Not once during Helen's sentence was her cell door locked. Warders were amongst the many who visited her for readings during her sentence. Other well-known supporters of the day included the British Prime Minister Winston Churchill, who was no stranger to psychic phenomena himself. Churchill is said to have visited Helen in prison on numerous occasions. But this was not the end of this sad story…

A police raid

In 1956, the year that Spiritualism was recognized as an official religion in Britain by an Act of Parliament, a séance was taking place in a Midlands home. Police had been alerted and rushed in and grabbed the medium, who was working with ectoplasm in a trance state at the time. The police were looking for signs of fraud like masks or false beards. They took endless photographs and the medium was given a humiliating strip search. Nothing at all was found to suggest fraud and it seems unbelievable that the police could have entered a private home in this way.

The medium was Helen Duncan and the shock of the raid caused the ectoplasm to return to her body too quickly. She was taken to hospital, where doctors discovered second-degree burns on her stomach. Tragically, she died just five weeks after this incident – a very sad end to a brilliant medium.

PHYSICAL MEDIUMSHIP

Physical mediumship involves physical objects moving or appearing as part of a séance. Not many mediums work with physical mediumship today. During the war years, blasting trumpets appeared in midair and ectoplasm appeared during séances!

Other phenomena of the séance room include direct voice, transfiguration and apports.

Direct voice

Direct voice mediums have the gift of bringing the voice of the deceased into the sitting. The spirits don't use the voicebox of the medium but a mouthpiece created from ectoplasm. (*See also Trance Mediumship.*)

Leslie Flint

One of the most tested direct voice mediums in recent times was Leslie Flint. Thousands of different voices were recorded during his séances, including many in languages that were unknown to Leslie himself. In his autobiography, *Voices in the Dark*, he described how he was bound up in every conceivable way and even *tested* with his mouth full of water. It never stopped the voices from coming!

Flint described his frustration with parapsychologists who even after many successful tests had been completed still seemed to have the intention of disproving the existence of life after death rather than proving it.

Transfiguration (overshadowing)

'Transfiguration' is a word commonly used nowadays to describe the phenomenon of seeing a spirit face appear over the top of a human host (the medium). Many people at a reading conducted in dim light will see their loved ones' faces appear to float over the face of the medium, sometimes slightly distorting it, often at the same time that messages are being brought through from the deceased. The medium's face can even momentarily take on the appearance of the deceased loved one.

Transfiguration in one form or another was taught more recently at the fictional wizard school Hogwarts in the Harry Potter books by J. K. Rowling, so it's likely you will have heard of it!

Faces in the mirror

Transfiguration in the modern-day meaning of faces appearing to float over the face of the medium is something you can actually try yourself if you want to – remembering my earlier warnings, of course (though no, I've never had a problem with this experience either).

You know at night-time when you walk into a room which is lit from behind, the windows are black and mirror-like? If you look into them and blur your vision slightly it seems as if a face appears over your own. (Of course some would argue this was the result of the distortion of the mirror!) This works pretty well and the only problem is that you find yourself both wanting to see it and being terrified in case it works. It's likely you never want to look into a mirror in the semi-darkness ever again, right?

Another method I have tried involves two or more people. You need a darkened room and a torch with red crepe paper over the glass so that the light shines through as red. One person sits in front of the rest of the group with the torch shining the red light on their face from below. If you look at their face you can see images appear over it, although you have to sit well back to do so.

Is this a trick of the light or your loved ones appearing to you? Who knows?

Apports/asports

An apport is the name given to a physical object, most commonly jewellery, money and flowers, which appears 'out of thin air' as a gift from a spirit visitor. These mainly appear in the presence of a medium. At the height of Spiritualism in the nineteenth century, they were one of the more common types of phenomenon at a séance.

Asports, on the other hand, are objects which *disappear* by psychic means, again usually during a séance.

Physical phenomena such as this can be useful evidence of spirit visitation, but it is wise to be aware that trickery might be performed too. A conjuror would be able to bring about both apports and asports in a convincing way.

Sathya Sai Baba

Sathya Sai Baba is an Indian 'miracle man' who regularly produces apports at his ashram in Puttaparti, India. People gather from all over the world to visit this mystical guru who appears to manifest objects from nowhere. Baba, who is always dressed in floor-length orange robes, is said to be an avatar (God incarnate) and has produced apports at will for his followers, often in front of hundreds of witnesses. Objects commonly include jewellery and coins, sometimes created on the spur of the moment and tailored to the requirements of the individual, making this very hard to put down to mere trickery. Baba also manifests a type of dust or ash called *vibhuthi*, which pours from his hands and appears on photographs and pictures of him.

I read with interest a piece on the website of medium and psychic Craig Hamilton-Parker about Sai Baba. He described how he'd been informed that the miracle man did not want people to write about him or promote him in articles. But then he opened a book at random and pointed to a page with a pin and the words under his pin confirmed that it 'was time' for the world to know about Baba. He took this as a sign that it was OK for him to publish his feature.

I decided to try this out for myself before adding this section about Sai Baba and opened a reference book on my desk at random. Pointing with the open end of a paperclip (I didn't have a handy pin!), I stabbed at the page beneath me. The quote was about Mikhail, or Michael, one of the four archangels of Islam. In my magazine columns I am known as 'The Angel Lady' and the quote underneath the paperclip jumped out at me. Mikhail is described as 'the *angel* who provides men with food and *knowledge*'. I guess I had my answer! I felt the message was that I was the 'angel' who would provide you with knowledge!

Like other forms of psychic phenomena, Sai Baba's psychic abilities are often surrounded by controversy, as is the man himself. You'll have to judge for yourself. But read up on him if you want to learn more about this fascinating man.

TRANCE MEDIUMSHIP/TRANCE CHANNELLING

Another form of mediumship is trance mediumship. Here the soul or spirit of the medium is pushed to one side (or sometimes lifted out of their body) momentarily whilst a spirit visitor borrows their body to communicate messages to the living. The medium often appears to fall asleep while the spirit visitor takes up residence and the spirit visitor is then able to animate the body and even talk in their own accent, dialect and even language (*see also Direct Voice*).

Often it is the medium's own spirit guide (*see below*) who controls the communications and spirit visitors and keeps the medium's physical body safe whilst the contact takes place. In most cases the medium will have no awareness of the contact and the communications that come through their body.

Having watched this phenomenon personally I have to say that the personality of the visiting spirit seems to completely alter the appearance of the human host – a difficult thing to fake! The human host really becomes the new personality. The popular English TV medium Colin Fry, host of the show *6ixth Sense with Colin Fry*, is an excellent example of a modern-day trance medium.

SPIRIT GUIDES/SPIRIT GUARDIANS

Each medium is different and works in their own way, but most work with a spirit helper of some sort, a spirit guide or guardian, sometimes called a 'control', who can act as a gatekeeper, rather like a nightclub bouncer, to the spirit realms.

In fact, as mentioned earlier, I believe we all have our own spiritual guides, even if we aren't aware of them. I feel that what we call our 'natural intuition' might well be messages which are filtering through to our conscious mind from the guides or guardian angels who are trying to direct us!

Guides are usually advanced human souls who act as teachers from the other realms. Traditionally, they show themselves as spiritual archetypes – monks, nuns and so on, or members of ancient spiritual groups of people like Native American tribes.

Other spirit counsellors who work closely with the living are the close relatives and friends we've known in life, like grandparents, although, as observed earlier, they might not prove to be very objective, as their natural instinct is to be protective! I have to say that not everyone agrees with this, but I have many case studies in my files where deceased parents and grandparents have stepped in with warnings for the loved ones they have left behind on Earth! Our relatives don't suddenly become all-seeing, all-knowing once they cross over to the heavenly side of life, but they do like to act as our 'guardian angels'! Some stories about this later...

VISITING A MEDIUM

Whether you visit a medium or not is very much a matter of personal choice. Mediums can bring great comfort and joy, but communication with the other side can be complicated and haphazard. Maybe this is why more and more souls are choosing to visit using their own methods – appearing in dreams and visions and bringing signs personally and directly to us. Why talk through a third party when you can speak direct?

Spontaneous afterlife contact contains few of the fears associated with other methods of contact. Contactees generally feel great joy after a spontaneous visitation, although it appears that not all spirits have the ability to communicate with the living in this way and not all of us are able to receive the messages.

If you do decide to visit with a medium, try to get a recommendation from a friend, or see if you can find a medium who is registered with an official body of some sort and follows a code of conduct. You can often find lists of mediums attached to Spiritualist churches (number in the telephone book) or you might choose to attend a service at a Spiritualist church. Your local new age shop might know of local experts or be able to recommend someone. Always use your own instincts to decide if this is the right course of action for you.

Even with an experienced medium, there are no guarantees that a message will come through for you. And even if you visit the same person over and over again, sometimes you might receive nothing at all in the way of contact. It's not always the fault of the medium – even the best mediums can have bad days too. Sometimes the energy of the spirit doesn't fit the personality of the reader and, as in life, personalities can clash and the reading can be a washout.

Many mediums do charge for their services; they give sittings as a business. There is nothing wrong with this, of course – we all have to eat and it is right to charge for one's time! Prices do vary a lot, though, so check before you book your appointment and ask about what is involved before you make your decision.

Last but not least, beware of the cold reader

Sadly, there are fraudulent people in the world and you may come across people who have little or no ability to communicate with spirits and whose only interest is in spiriting away your money. The grieving are especially open to trickery, such is the longing to make contact with the other side. Make no mistake – I *am* a firm believer in the afterlife, but by the law of averages not all 'psychic readers' are going to be genuine.

There is a technique called 'cold reading' which involves the 'medium' passing along a lot of generalities and repeating back names which you yourself have mentioned earlier in the sitting (it's very easy to forget what you have said).

Examples of cold reading might include things such as, 'I hear a name of an older female relative… The name begins with "J". Yes, "J". Does this mean anything to you?' Is the relative dead or alive? Many names begin with the letter 'J' of course! The fraudulent 'medium' then might suggest a string of names, watching your face and body language until they hit upon one that fits. 'It sounds like Jo, Joan, Jane, Janet, Julie, Jenny … something like that…'

Eager to please, the sitter might start suggesting names. 'Could it be Jackie?'

The medium will be quick to respond. 'Yes, Jackie – ah yes, I hear it now, it's Jackie … of course.'

It would be easy to consider this a *hit*, even though the 'medium' has actually given you nothing at all!

Also beware of generalities such as 'They're telling me that you are often misunderstood by others [who isn't?], you work so hard and no one appreciates you as they should [who doesn't agree with that?], you sometimes struggle with money [what does that mean exactly? Everyone wants more money than they have], you'd like to do better at work and feel underpaid [we all feel underpaid, right?], you could be doing more with your life [oh yes, indeed!] and they will help you [can you prove that?].'

Sometimes cold readers will use 'common' names, depending on your culture, age and so on, in the hope of getting a hit and then spend ages on generalities around this one person without mentioning if they are alive or dead, old, young, a friend or relative, a friend of a friend or even someone you know vaguely from work! The fraudster doesn't care one bit!

There *are* some amazing and accurate mediums out there, so don't let me completely dampen your enthusiasm, but do be aware of the possible negative consequences before making your choice and don't forget to do your research first of all! A genuine medium will have no problem with you taping the session so that you can examine the facts after the event. After all, a genuine medium is going to get recommendations and future business.

TABLE TIPPING

There are many ways in which you can communicate with spirits apart from through a medium, of course. Table tipping is one of them. This was a very popular pastime in the early home séance. It provided one way in which the sitters could become involved in the action, although initially it was considered nothing more than a parlour game. Small, light tables were frequently used for the experiment, sometimes with wheels on their feet so that they would be able to move easily. Often a cloth was placed over the table to discourage people from pushing or moving it, as this would be more noticeable with a cloth under their fingers! Then the participants would each place their fingertips or flat palms on the table alongside those of the medium and the energy of the spirit visitors would be used to move the table and tip it about.

Some believe table tipping occurs as a result of group human consciousness rather than spirit contact. It certainly seems to be true that the more an individual group practises the activity, the more the table seems to move about! In time participants can also be rewarded by rapping and knocking sounds, which are often followed by vibrations and the tipping or moving of the table.

Apparently table tipping, like many psychic phenomena, works best in near-dark conditions, although I have to say, apart from the face transfiguration exercises, I can see no reason to work in the dark – unless you are up to no good, right? Really, it works just as well in the light (unless you are going for a spooky effect or trying to scare yourself, which is a little pointless).

Rapping codes can be developed to enable sitters to 'communicate' with the deceased (like the Fox sisters did), with different numbers of knocks indicating chosen letters, words or phrases. This is an awkward and clumsy method of communicating with your loved ones, in my opinion, but it is easily repeatable.

With any form of spirit communication, you should always ask for proof of who your communicator is if you can. Ask questions of the spirits, just to be sure.

OUIJA BOARDS/TALKING BOARDS/SPIRIT BOARDS/ANGEL BOARDS

Ouija boards (from the French and German words for 'yes')

were created initially as parlour games. Made of card or thin strips of wood, the boards traditionally contain the letters of the alphabet and the words 'Yes' and 'No', although more complicated versions also exist. Using a planchette (which translates as 'little plank') or 'pointer', sitters can spell out words and phrases supposedly communicated from the spirit realms. Sitting in a circle around the board, each person places a finger on the pointer. After questions have been asked of the spirits, the pointer will begin to move, spelling out answers from those on the other side. Another variation of this communication was called 'Ask the Glass' (naturally using a glass to spell out the words).

From the 1890s onwards, dozens of manufacturers began producing intricate and beautifully illustrated talking boards for both 'family fun' and spirit communication, but the frightening phenomena which occurred when they were wrongly used soon meant that they gained a bad name.

Angel boards are slightly different. They are so called because of their angelic illustrations, although the letters and numbers that illustrate them are done in much the same way. It is thought that the intent of those using these particular boards is to communicate with higher levels of spirit energies and guides, although the method is very similar to communicating with spirits.

I have worked with several types of boards, using special protection and under strict conditions, of course, and I have to say that I have experienced extraordinary and mainly positive results, but it has to be said that it is easy to become addicted to such communication.

It would be wrong of me not to give this warning. My extensive postbag occasionally contains letters from distressed people who have used spirit boards for amusement whilst under the influence of alcohol or drugs and without using psychic protection as might be performed by an experienced medium, including prayers. So if you intend using these boards, do take care.

Other experiences can be more positive, however. Sue e-mailed to tell me she had been using an angel board, then later e-mailed again with an update. I thought you might find it useful reading:

Communication via an angel board

I e-mailed you in January to tell you about our trials with the angel board communicator. I just wanted to let you know that we have used the board twice since then and both times we had brilliant contact with our loved ones.

We made contact with my sister's other daughter, who had always hung back in making contact through mediums. The board is so amazing, but when you tell people they kind of look at you in a strange way. However, we will continue to tell people about the joy of the afterlife.

Last weekend my daughter also joined in. She is a believer anyway, but even though I had told her how the glass moved she had not imagined just how fast it went. Last weekend she had a fantastic message from her granddad, who incidentally was a non-believer on the Earth plane. We also had messages from my sister's two girls, plus my dear friend Jackie.

It is amazing how the individuals' sense of humour is apparent even though we are communicating through letters and a glass.

We did have a bit of a weird contact who would not confirm who they were, even though we were asking them either to identify whom they knew at the table or to spell out their name. In fact we got the sense this spirit had a nasty side. We were not sure what to do, so I asked them to leave via the 'X' (we ask all the spirits to exit that way when they are ready to go). We have found that once contact has been made, most of the sitters' fingers cannot keep up with the glass anyway! We do want to be respectful to our spirit friends.

These lovely ladies had wonderful and positive experiences on the board, as I have done myself. But negative and frightening experiences *can* result when these boards are handled incorrectly. Even sometimes when you do use them correctly, uninvited spirits will try and communicate.

People have reported objects being thrown about and terrifying predictions being made of unpleasant deaths. I've never seen this myself, though, and to be fair, most of these stories come from groups of teenagers. You have been warned. But I have to tell you this does *not* reflect my experiences!

Bear in mind manufacturer Parker Brothers' slogan about the boards: 'It's only a game – isn't it?'

SPIRIT WRITING/AUTOMATIC WRITING

The process of spirit writing or automatic writing needs only a writing instrument and a pad of paper, along with a willing human scribe. A modern version might include a computer screen and keyboard. The writer holds the pen and writes in the normal way but the communications come from spirits and do not pass through the writer's conscious mind. Usually they are aware of the act of writing, but not usually of the messages which appear on the paper (on occasion this method can be performed whilst the 'medium' is in a trance state). Some people will even use the opposite hand to their 'normal' writing hand to 'channel' the messages.

Channelled messages are fairly easy for many people to bring through and many books are said to have been written by spirits working though their human instruments in this way. Some people do suggest that there is a danger to this form of contact with the spirit realms, but I'm not sure how exactly – haunted by a pen?

Early Spiritualists developed fancy pen-holders (a basket/cradle type of affair) and the mediums had simply to rest their hand on the basket to establish contact. (*See also Ouija Boards.*)

I had a go at spirit writing once with two friends. The three of us, all experienced mediums, tried to hold a pen at the same time – difficult but possible! We managed to get images as well as readable words and with practice got better at this.

Once when one of my cats went missing I asked for help from the other side using this method. The results were a drawing of a simple map and a location marked with an 'X'. The place shown was across local fields. At the time crops were growing and even though I tried I could not get to the location that had been marked. The cat was missing for four weeks, yet he was eventually found in the place marked by the 'X' on the map which had been drawn for me.

I do believe that, as with the other methods of communication mentioned here, there is some intelligence at work and the contact could well come from our own family of loving spirits or our guardian angel or spirit guide. Fascinating!

ELECTRONIC VOICE PHENOMENON: EVP

The phrase 'Electronic Voice Phenomenon' was coined in the 1970s by the publishers Colin Smythe Ltd. The phenomenon is said to be the voices of discarnate entities appearing on recording media. In most cases the recordings contain just one or two words, which are mainly unclear, although success can vary. References to EVP have appeared in many recent films and TV programmes, for example *Supernatural*, *White Noise* and *The Sixth Sense*.

If you want to have a go at this in its simplest form, place a recording device in an empty room and leave it alone to record your messages. It doesn't particularly matter what sort of device you use – even an old tape recorder might work. If you wish, you can ask questions on the tape and leave a blank space for answers. Of course you need to be aware that it is easy to pick up your neighbour's dog barking, people talking in the street outside and so on.

Spirit communication does appear to be becoming more and more sophisticated with the advent of modern technology and EVP is particularly intriguing. Perhaps it's just me, but I'm sure spirits are trying to reach us this way, although you have to be open-minded to interpret some of the 'evidence' gathered.

Recently new and improved methods of spirit communication are appearing using telephones. Here's a great example:

A sister talks on a mobile phone – from the other side

Karen, a visitor to my website, recently sent me an e-mail to explain that she and her daughter had inadvertently recorded the voice of her dead sister on her mobile phone.

She told me that her daughter Sam was teasing her because her voice sounded particularly low one day. She was joking that she was going to use the voice recorder on her mobile phone to record her mother's 'manly voice'.

Karen explains:

So she set it up and the house phone rang almost right away. I answered it whilst Sam went off to have a shower. When I finished the call I sat down to watch television and some time later Sam came and joined me in the living room. She picked up her mobile phone and complained that her battery level was now showing only one bar of charge left, even though she'd fully charged up her phone that morning.

Sam then proceeded to play back the recording and you could hear me in the background chatting on the house phone and Sam telling me she was off for a shower (which in fact I didn't hear at the time). Then the recording went silent for a few seconds and my sister Anne was heard to say, "I'm here, Karen!" Yet Anne passed with cancer over six years ago!

Karen told me that both she and her daughter were 100 per cent certain that the voice belonged to Anne and they were both greatly comforted by the fact that she was still around them.

ORBS AND OTHER PHOTOGRAPHIC ANOMALIES

What is an orb? It's a ball of light which appears on photographic film. There may be a fair number of explanations for this phenomenon, including mist, dust, sunspots, insects and smoke, but there are some balls and flashes of light which seem to defy explanation.

Some people believe the lights are spirit communicators and I've personally seen photographs where the faces of deceased relatives seem to appear on family wedding photographs. Sometimes a light appears above the space where the deceased might have sat at the wedding table, for example. One photograph I have seen shows the silhouette of a woman appearing in a window. The family had invited their mother, who'd died the previous year, to attend their Christmas dinner celebrations and they were convinced she was showing herself via the image in the glass.

In one newspaper article, an orb which appeared on a photograph above a young girl was digitally enhanced by specialists employed by the paper. After that, a face could clearly be seen in the orb, and the family, who had no prior knowledge that the newspaper was going to be working on the image in this way, instantly recognized it as that of the child's dead grandmother.

I've seen a lot of these photographs and I do find them intriguing, although I'm not a scientist and have never tested photographs sent to me in any way. Have a look though photographs in your own family album – you might be surprised at what you find!

One of my daughters and I were having fun with a camera at home one day. She took stacks of photographs of me, one after the other. Eventually, growing tired of this, I snatched the camera off her and just for fun asked her to pose with her (dead) uncle. (He's a regular spirit visitor in our home!) Expecting nothing out of the ordinary, we were stunned when we downloaded the photographs onto the family computer. No light phenomenon appears on any of the photographs my daughter took of me, but on the one where I asked her to pose with her dead uncle, there is a large orb! It may mean nothing, but then again…?

You know I have to say, though: be careful not to get too carried away by this. I get sent a lot of photographs and people e-mail me to say 'Look at this amazing photograph of late Uncle Bill' or whatever. Try as I might, in most cases, Uncle Bill just looks like a smudge or a bit of mist to me. Maybe I am being unkind?

I guess to sum up I would have to say that overall, yes, I believe that there is something to this, but not every photographic orb is going to be the image of a deceased relative. Use common sense.

MORE ABOUT VISITATIONS

It's lovely to receive communication and support from our loved ones in the other world, but we should try not to become dependent on it. It is easy to become addicted to psychic readings and the same problem might arise with dream visitations if our loved ones appear too readily.

Support is wonderful, but part of living is to actually *live*. That means learning and growing from our own experiences ... and mistakes. Yes, I know that sounds mean, but you know in your heart it's true.

Your loved ones want to show you that they support your choices – whatever they are. Sometimes there is no right or wrong way forward in life. There might be many pathways and it doesn't matter which we choose. What matters is that we decide and that we make choices that are right for us at the time. OK, to be fair, I've noticed in some visitation experiences our loved ones can and do give us little clues! I bet they get into trouble, though...

Rachel's dad came to show his support in a dream visitation:

A comforting hug

Two nights after my dad had passed away, he came to me in a dream. I said to him, 'What are you doing here? You're meant to be dead!' He then said that he loved me and wanted to give me a hug, which he did.

I cried in his arms, not wanting to let go, and woke up sobbing.

A few weeks later he came to me again in my dreams and said that I had to let him go as he couldn't visit me so often, but I didn't want him to leave me and again I woke up sobbing and felt abandoned by him.

I do still dream of him, but now they are comforting dreams where he comes to me and gives me the hug that I desperately want from him. And sometimes it's as if he hasn't gone and he's still included in my normal dreams.

I get whiffs of his aftershave every now and then, and when I think of him (still every day) I get a reminder of him, like the Carpenters' songs that he loved and that we played at his crematorium service.

Will asking your loved ones to contact you work? I can't say for sure, but if you feel that is something you'd like to try, then have a go.

One lady gave this a try. She was desperate to contact her parents, but was disappointed when they did appear to her. Her mother stepped forward in a dream visitation and said to her, 'What do you want? Why have you bothered us?' Not a pleasant reaction, you'll agree! This writer did explain to me that she had never got along with her parents in life and didn't like them much anyway. It seems that nothing had changed now that they had moved on. To be honest, I'm not sure why she bothered trying to contact them in the first place.

Thankfully, this sort of reaction is rare, but it is important to share all sides of the story so that if you decide to try this for yourself you are prepared.

Here is a more positive example. Although it happened to a teenager, don't for one minute feel that it is made up or insincere in any way. It follows the classic pattern of visitation and is a great example of what *can* happen … if you ask.

'Granddad came after I asked him'

I am just 13 years old and last night my mother took me to buy one of your books. It really inspired me and made me laugh and cry. Even though I only started reading last night, I'm on page 137 already.

Just before I went to sleep I was explaining to my dad how I wished I could visit granddad one last time. Then later during the night I had the most amazing dream. In it my father and I met up with my granddad. I was hugging Granddad and telling him how much I loved him, and even though he didn't seem able to reply or put his arms round me, he stood still and gave me a massive smile!

I know Granddad came to me because he knew I wouldn't be scared any more.

Black-and-white variations

My sister told me once that when my father-in-law visited her in a dream to bring her messages for me, he appeared to her in black and white, even though the background was in colour. He chatted with her for quite a while, so I wondered if appearing in black and white meant that he would be able to stick around for longer. Maybe black and white took up less energy? Was it more important to sacrifice the colour and stay around long enough to be able to answer questions, which is what he did with her? I'd never heard about a visiting spirit appearing in black and white before. Perhaps it had happened, though, and no one had thought to mention it.

The very next morning I was stunned to receive an e-mail about a visitation experience in black and white. I'd been studying visitations for years and then there were two references to black-and-white ones in 24 hours… Even for me, this was weird!

'What are the chances of that happening?' I asked my sister when we chatted on the phone later on.

'Fairly high, actually!' she laughed.

She was probably right. And I guess my own 'family of spirits' had something to do with it.

I'll share the black-and-white story with you. It comes from England and shows the problems we have when our religious belief gets in the way of loving and comforting messages.

Black and white

Well, where do I start? I'm a 30-year-old mother of two boys and have been married for 10 years. I've always worked as a health-care assistant and have dealt with death as part of my work for many years. In the past I have seen silhouettes of people, heard unusual things and sensed things too, but I always dismissed it because I believe in God and I thought it was bad to believe in spirits too. I realize now that's not true. God seems to help people to receive messages.

I lost my dear dad on New Year's Eve and my world came crashing down. I've saved so many lives but I couldn't save my own dad. Every day for two weeks before the funeral I would cry out to Dad, saying, 'Just let me know you are OK. Please show me a sign, then I can be strong.' I even told the vicar what I'd said, but he didn't agree with it.

On the day of the funeral we went to my brother's house. Everyone was there, including family members I'd never met. Before we left for the funeral I wanted to use the toilet, but when I went upstairs the door was closed. I knocked and no one answered, so I then called out and tried the door. It was locked, so I waited. An aunt I didn't know came up the stairs and I explained that someone was in there and I thought perhaps whoever it was needed a few moments to themselves. We chatted for a while about my dad, then my sister-in-law came up too. I told her we were waiting, but I have to say I was getting desperate now, so I called out again and still no one answered.

Just to check in case I had been mistaken, I pulled the handle down and was pushing the door when a voice said, 'It's me.' It sounded a little like my brother, so I guessed he was trying to compose himself. My aunt and sister-in-law and I all heard him speak.

We decided to go downstairs and wait so as not to embarrass him, but as I walked into the kitchen I saw him sitting at the table! I started to panic and looked around to make sure everyone else was downstairs. When I realized they were, I began to cry and explain to my brother why I was upset. Who was in the bathroom?

My brother calmed me down and we went upstairs together, but the door was now open and no one was there. After that I was no longer afraid and just started laughing. At least I'd had my sign from Dad!

I thanked Dad and after that I saw his outline several times. I could smell his aftershave too, but I still found it hard that he had gone.

Another night I was woken by a kiss on the side of my mouth. I thought it was my husband, then realized he was asleep beside me. I closed my eyes, then I started to see my dad and he was smiling. He appeared to me in black and white, and I was saying in my head, 'I can see you, Dad, I can see you.' It was all over in a few minutes. I have never seen, heard or smelled my dad from that day on, so I guess I had what I'd needed.

In a visitation dream it is sometimes possible to literally feel your visiting loved one, as in this story. They can hold your hand, put a hand on your shoulder or give you a hug. The experience feels very real. One lady told me that her husband explained to her that he could hug her but that they wouldn't be able to hug for long because it took a lot of energy to maintain the hug.

Nick told me that he had regular visits from a family friend. He always appeared as a solid full-colour figure. On his last visit, however, he explained that it was possible for them to touch, but he would be unable to touch him and see him at the same time! Nick said that his friend then disappeared, but he held his hand and his arm before he woke up.

(See chapters 7–9 for many more wonderful afterlife visitation experiences.)

CHAPTER 5

Helping Us through Grief

*I am well aware that many will say that no one
can possibly speak with spirits and angels so long
as he lives in the body; and many will say that it
is all fancy, others that I relate such things in order
to gain credence, and others will make other
objections.*

EMANUEL SWEDENBORG

One of the main reasons spirits visit, as we have seen, is to
help us through our grief by showing us that they are OK
now.

Research into the effects of grief is ongoing for me.
During some Internet searches I strayed across the Net
Doctor website (www.netdoctor.co.uk) and was interested
to read an article written by Dr P. J. Marshall and research

specialist registrar in psychiatry Clare Atkinson. The article discusses grief, bereavement and depression and lists seeing and hearing the voice of the deceased as 'common experiences' (although it doesn't say whether the authors thought these were delusional experiences or real ones). Other common experiences include disturbed sleep, anger, guilt and obsession with the deceased – things that parallel my own research relating to grief alongside esoteric experiences.

A GRIEF SPECIALIST'S OPINION

I wanted to learn more about how paranormal experiences affected the grieving and got in contact with grief specialist Darcie D. Sims, PhD, CHT, CT, GMS. Darcie is also a bereaved parent and child, grief management specialist, director of the *American Grief Academy* in Seattle, Washington, and the author of many related books. She is the voice of experience, as she lost her son 31 years ago to a malignant brain tumour. She says at that time there was very little in the way of information or support for bereaved parents and she swore that if she got through her pain she would do something about it. She has now been doing grief work for 26 years.

Darcie told me:

I am a licensed clinical hypnotherapist and have often had clients who have experienced many things that defy explanation in the normal *sense – whatever* normal *means! I too have a deep spiritual connection and believe that more is possible than the human mind can embrace, so I am truly interested in your work. As a bereaved parent and child, I have had my own experiences which have no reasonable explanation, but they did occur, so I now simply believe in the wonders of a world I do not have to understand in order to receive its benefits and gifts.*

I think people get stuck in their grief because they do not have adequate and accurate information about the grieving process and what it is… No one really knows what it is, although there is a lot of research about what it should *be! Everyone has their own unique timetable for the process and no one should be forced, shoved or even encouraged to speed it up. It is a natural process, with many ups and downs, resembling waves washing up on a beach. Some come crashing down on us while others merely tickle the toes, but each has a purpose and a value.*

I think we sometimes hold on to the pain of our grief far longer than perhaps we need to because we are afraid that the pain is the only remaining link we have with our loved one. How wrong we are! You don't stop loving someone just because they die. We are forever linked through our love. Our loved ones are threads in our fabric, to be rewoven again and again throughout our life, as wonderful parts of who we are.

Moving on has little meaning for the bereaved, but I believe the non-bereaved mean that we should put our sorrow away and try to get back to our 'old self'. Returning to who we were is impossible, as we are someone new now ... and we will create a new 'normal' for ourselves. We cannot return to the 'old us', but we can move forward, bringing with us all the wonder, joys and sorrows of our relationship with our loved one. We can transform the relationship, but not abandon it. I am still Big A's mother and always will be, but I no longer save for his college education. Closure is a media word, meaning we are moving on to the next story, but my story will continue to be written with my son's memory and life intertwined with mine!

I was interested to know if, as a *traditional* grief expert with many years' experience of working with the bereaved, Darcie had encountered any paranormal experiences relating to grief and what her thoughts on them might be. She told me:

I have heard many, many stories from clients and families over the last 26 years. In every instance, their experiences were positive and they felt both relief *that their loved one was OK and* love *flowing from their loved one. They were also, in most cases, quite reluctant to tell anyone about their experiences as they believed that most people would think them 'crazy'.*

I had one experience of my own that left me feeling warm, loved and very, very comforted. Many years ago, early in my own grief, I was visited by our son. I was sitting in his rocking chair, trying to relax, when I suddenly was aware that he was in my arms. He was a young child when he died of a malignant brain tumour and his entire life had been a horrible battle. I did not question the moment, but simply enjoyed being able to hold him again and rock, as we had done many times. I was filled with a sense of overwhelming peace and seemed to hear him telling me he was OK now and that I should be OK too.

I have no idea how long that lasted, but it was enough to convince me that I could go forward with my life and know he was whole and healed. I am not a religious person but am quite spiritual and this was a choice point in my grief journey. I moved from always remembering his death to remembering first that he had lived, and that has made all the difference to my life.

Darcie had another family experience that she was kind enough to share:

Our daughter Alicia (Allie) experienced a visit from her brother when she was 16 and on a canoeing adventure with the Girl Scouts in the far northern Canadian wilderness. At one point during her two-

week trip her canoe was tossed into some huge rocks during a sudden storm. She was thrown from the canoe, hit the rocks and began to sink. The canoe was swamped and lost. She remembers being under the water, with blood flowing from a head wound, and telling her brother that she was not afraid to die, but that she didn't think Mom could take having her die too. Then she remembers being lifted up and gently placed on the rocky shoreline. Her canoeing partner remembers seeing her nearly fly through the air as a huge wave tossed her onto the rocky beach. Allie remembers being hugged and gently lifted to the beach. She knows it was her brother who helped her.

I asked Darcie how she felt that spontaneous afterlife contact assisted the healing of grief. She told me:

As a psychologist and pragmatic thinker, I of course want clear, concise data and proof of such things. Since those are not available and yet it is clear that my own experience and my daughter's were real and those of others who have shared their experiences with me were also real, I have no choice but to remain open and receptive to things that do not need explaining! I have not encountered anyone who was hurt or terrified by these experiences. In fact, they were comforted by them and experienced great warmth and a sense of peace. Since I also experienced that, I am no longer in any doubt that there are many things that we cannot explain but that are no less real *than those things we can explain or account for in a tangible manner. I am a believer and respect what I do not understand but have experienced.*

Darcie also told me more about love and grieving and what she calls 'choice points':

Grief is such an individual journey that it seems inappropriate to attempt to put fences, borders and expectation around it. Grief is the price we pay for love, and if we have loved, then it makes perfect sense that we will hurt when that love is no longer within hug's reach. What I know more than anything is that even though death comes, love never goes away.

There are choice points *in our grief journey and one of them arrives when you must decide whether you will forever concentrate on the loss or whether you will allow the love to return. May love be what you remember the most.*

(*See the Further Information section for more information about Darcie's work.*)

MEN'S GRIEF

Thomas Golden, LCSW, is well known in the field of healing from loss. His book *Swallowed by a Snake: The Gift of the Masculine Side of Healing* has been acclaimed by the grief specialist Elisabeth Kübler-Ross and others.

I asked Thomas why he felt that men in particular find it difficult to move on after loss. He told me:

Everyone is different. Because our culture gives us very few rituals to help with the processing of grief we are left to our own devices and this leaves people wondering how much grief is enough – or too much. Grief is tricky. Sometimes people become identified with the grief and it becomes a part of them rather than something that passes through them.

He explained that men and women's grief were different: 'After a major loss women often move towards a nurturing and intimate connection and men move towards *doing* something.'

Interestingly enough, with my own work I haven't noticed a difference particularly between the numbers of men who have paranormal experiences and the numbers of women, although women tend to share their experiences more – and tell me about the paranormal experiences their husbands and partners have!

I was interested to find out if Thomas had come across paranormal phenomena at all, especially amongst his work with men. He said, 'Probably about a quarter of the people I have seen have had experiences with sensing the presence of their deceased loved ones. That's a guess. They range from just a feeling to full-blown visions.'

I asked him his opinion of the spontaneous afterlife communication experience in relation to healing, and he felt such experiences might be useful: 'They can be an integral part of a person's sense of the dead person and therefore can be instrumental in helping people to shift their consciousness.'

(*See the Further Information section for more information about Tom's work.*)

FEELING BAD – MORE THINGS WHICH HOLD US BACK

Life after loss is the most enormous struggle for us. Our loved ones' lives are so interwoven with our own that we don't just miss their presence, we miss their everyday interaction in our lives both right now and in the future we shall never have together. Bereavement is a complicated issue. We mourn how we'd share jokes and laugh and cry together. Every funny story now hangs in the air. Some things are only funny when shared with another.

Every disagreement suddenly seems pointless. If we fall out with someone before they die we always have immediate regrets, saying, 'I never got the opportunity to make it up,' and we carry the burden of knowing that that opportunity will never come again.

Some people feel bad because they were unable to be with their loved ones during their final moments of life. Yet no one can be with every single loved one when their moment comes to leave the Earth plane. In many cases death can be unexpected and even when months or weeks of notice are given as the soul slowly slips from the body we still can't always be there. People write and tell me, 'I sat by the bed for days at a time, rarely getting any sleep or anything to eat, and yet the moment I was persuaded to go and get a sandwich, my father died…' They feel cheated, which is pointless. I believe that relatives sometimes choose to depart at that time – a final moment of privacy or perhaps a choice to somehow save those closest to them the pain of that last breath.

I once heard the saying 'It's not how you die that counts, it's how you live your life,' and I agree. The American TV medium John Edward talks about loving, honouring and respecting the living and he is right. We are only human, after all, and if we feel we have made mistakes with someone in life, rather than waste time on a lesson unlearned, we need to take that example and replay it in another person's life, someone still living. Work harder at interaction with those that are still here – it's the best way to honour the death of another.

My mother always says, 'I don't want flowers when I'm dead,' and what she means is 'I'd rather have them when I'm alive' – a good point and one that we do remember!

MOVING THROUGH GUILT

Guilt, as we've seen, is a common emotion after a death. Here are some of the reasons why people feel guilty after a loss:

- They have the feeling that they could have done more to help the person in life.

- They feel that they could have spent more time with the person when they were dying.

- They feel horror that they were not with their loved one when they passed.

- They feel that they could have somehow prevented the death of their loved one.

- They feel guilty about angry feelings they had about the person whilst they were alive.

- They feel guilty about angry feelings that they have about their loved one now they are dead.

- They worry that they have not avenged the person's death.

- They feel that they should have done more at the funeral, or to help their relatives and friends, or guilty over the way they organized their possessions – pretty well everything, actually!

******

From a paranormal perspective, the spirits of our loved ones are often aware of these feelings. It is important that they pull back at this time to enable the healing of our own souls. Sometimes this doesn't seem to happen and I have a lot of case histories where the soul visits the living to assist in this healing process. But this can work too. People tell me, 'As soon as I saw him in my dream and knew he was OK, I felt better and was able to carry on living my life,' or 'I felt so bad about everything that had happened, I was torturing myself all the time, telling myself that I should be doing more, but when I felt him around me I knew it was going to be OK.'

Our deceased loved ones do want to show that they are aware of our efforts and to reassure us. Here is a good example of this:

Rest in peace

Nine months after my dad passed away I was in a lot of turmoil and suffering the effects of what I called 'emotional healing'. My son Lee, who is now 32, lost his dad when he was five. He had had an industrial illness and I had fought hard to try to prove negligence, without success. I think my dad dying brought back some of the turmoil from my earlier loss, which I have read can happen.

I was having a restless night and had already got up to go to the bathroom. When I climbed into bed I lay there in a half-awake, half-dream state and a strange 'vision' slowly came towards me … floating. I felt as if I was suspended in time but was completely in awe during the experience. As the vision came closer I was surrounded by a golden light. I recognized the outline as a gold-threaded gown with large bell sleeves. Around the head area there was a glowing golden circle and in the middle of this circle was my late husband's face as he had been in life just before he passed. He was smiling, but it was like a photo that I have of him. The next thing I remember is waking and hearing the words in my head: 'Rest in peace.'

I knew instinctively that I was being told to 'let go' and stop stressing as I had been in the hope of finding some compensation for Lee.

I know that it was a vision and not a dream, as it was so vivid and unlike anything I had ever experienced before! It was as if it was in my mind's eye but it felt as if it was in the room because it came right up to my right side.

I got up a few days later at 6.30 a.m. and was actually compelled to write four pages to Lee explaining what had happened, but I never gave it to him because I know he is sceptical of these things! I was in floods of tears and felt cleansed afterwards and have never felt any anguish about it since. I have told my mum and sister, who believe me, as my mum had a near-death experience years ago.

TALKING TO THE BEREAVED – WHAT TO SAY AND DO

When my husband's mother died in tragic circumstances many years ago, I remember people literally crossing the road rather than approach us. Most people are so frightened of saying the wrong thing. They don't talk to you at all. Later people would approach me and ask me, 'How is he?' rather than talk to John directly. Fear of 'getting it wrong' means that people do nothing.

So what do the bereaved need from those around them?

- Someone to listen. Words of comfort can often be meaningless, but listening will always help. Some people will want to talk almost immediately and others may take weeks or months to want to do this, if at all. Be ready if and when that time comes. You don't have to answer every question, or even any question. 'Why?' might not have an answer.

- Be open to all the bereaved person's thoughts, feelings and experiences. This can be particularly important if they have experienced something paranormal. It doesn't matter what your own thoughts and feelings about the experience are – just listen! In 99 per cent of these cases the experience will be a positive one and the grieving just want you to acknowledge that it was very real (even if you only believe it was 'real for them'). Your own spiritual beliefs don't need to be compromised at all. Just listen.

- How long do you stay? Don't stay too long. Take your cue from the bereaved and leave when appropriate. Keeping in regular contact is usually more important. Most people stop 'being there' after what they consider a suitable time of mourning and yet most people want to talk about their loved ones many years after those around them feel they should have 'moved on'. Also, paranormal experiences can happen at any time from just before the death to many years afterwards.

  Something to consider: on occasion people have dream visitations from people they have met or known in their distant past. This spirit might have come to inform them that they have died. Paranormal experiences related to death don't necessarily have to be associated with grief itself and can happen at any time!

- Don't compare your loss or experiences with theirs. Each person will have the grief experience that is right for them.

- Children experience loss very differently from adults. They are more likely to experience paranormal phenomena in a more vivid way. A child will see Grandma sitting on the bed, for example, talking and looking very similar to the way she did before death (but at her healthiest). If children feel that those around them might be upset about their visitation experiences, they might not share them, yet acknowledgement of these experiences can be very healing for the child as well as for others.

******

ANNIVERSARIES

Maybe it is because the first anniversary of a death can be so painful that this is when so many people experience paranormal incidents associated with their lost loved one. Other occasions are birthdays, weddings, births and other important family events. You are more likely to sense your loved ones around you at these times.

Typical anniversary experiences are similar to those that might occur at other times:

- You see a symbol or sign which was special to the deceased.

- On your special day your song or their song plays within your hearing.

- You smell their perfume or aftershave.

- You sense them with you.

- You bump into someone you associate with them.

******

Julie told me about her family experience:

Happy Christmas

On the 30 September my dad passed away from cancer. I was at the hospital when he died, as were my two daughters, Carlye, 16, and Becky, 13.

Since his passing Becky has experienced many 'dreams' in which she also 'dies' and finds that her granddad is waiting for her. They sit and chat in a place that Becky calls heaven.

Before Christmas, Becky had a dream experience where she took all of her presents with her and opened them with her granddad in heaven. Rather bizarrely, the gifts she opened in her dream experience were the actual gifts that we had bought her here on Earth – and there is no way she could have known about any of them!

She dreams about him so much. When my mum was ill recently we were all worried that we might lose her too, but my dad came to Becky and said we were not to worry, as she was going to be OK and wouldn't be joining him for a long time.

Becky's 'death' is of course a symbol to indicate that she has visited an alternative reality, in this case heaven.

Elizabeth's visitor came to her when she needed it most:

An extra guest at the wedding

My mam died in 1980 and there were many times when I felt I needed her. I always wished she would send me a message to tell me that everything was going to be all right.

Then in 1994 I met my husband-to-be, John. I knew from the start that Mam would have thought the world of him. I had three girls and every time I gave birth I wished with all my heart that my mam would come and show herself. She never did, but with my first birth my daughter and I nearly died. I was also very ill with the other two births and somehow I believed that my mam was looking after me each time. Even though I didn't actually see her or feel her at all, I just knew.

In 2001 John and I married, and I really wanted my mam to see how happy I was. Even though I'd felt she'd been with me in the past, this was different. This was my wedding.

As I stood waiting to go into church, I just broke down. I wanted my mam to be with me more than I had ever wanted anything in the previous 20 years. Eventually, when I had calmed down enough (and was late for my wedding), I walked into the church and had the most overwhelming feeling of love that I had ever felt in my life. As I stood at the altar someone touched me on my back and I actually turned around to see who it was. Everyone, including my small children, was sitting down and nobody was anywhere near me.

I know that two things happened then: Mam showed me that she was at my wedding and secondly, more importantly, she approved!

Here's another story, this time from Wales. Did Carol's nan influence her decision to visit this particular day or was it a coincidence? Did she somehow sense something that led her to an important date?

An important birthday

I was walking past the cemetery on a beautiful summer's morning early in August of this year when I had the sudden impulse to go in and visit my nan's unmarked grave. She died when I was 16 and I can count how many times on one hand I have visited her grave side since her passing, but that day I felt drawn for some reason.

I feel I should mention at this point that even though my nan lived with me until I was nine, we didn't really have a loving relationship. My mother and my nan were more like enemies, and I was brought up to know that, and I guess I sided with my mother, which I now feel bad about.

I felt very peaceful and contented walking around the graveyard, really at one with myself. When I found my nan's grave I stood there for quite a while, thinking of her.

Later that day I told my sister that I had been to visit her grave and she said, 'How strange – it would have been her 100th birthday today!' I had had no idea!

After that day, I found my nan was on my mind a lot. After 27 years, I was actually missing her. I even felt a little tearful thinking of her, which surprised me!

Then a few weeks later my sister came round to a family gathering and brought with her a pile of old photographs of Nan as a young woman and my dad as a child. She handed me one. It was just my nan on her own. On the back she had written a poem, which read:

> *Think of me when the Gold Sun is sinking*
> *And your heart from care set free.*
> *Whilst of others you are thinking,*
> *Will you sometimes think of me?*

I was taken aback, especially when I read the last line. It gave me goose pimples. I felt it really meant something to me and me alone. I think I was meant to read those words. It was as if my nan was aware that she had been on my mind.

CHILDREN'S EXPERIENCES

For many children going though grief, the death is their

first-ever experience of loss. They might not understand what being dead means or what happens next. They might think of nothing else and become clingy and confused.

Having said that, it is my experience that children more easily accept paranormal experiences related to the loss, especially when the visit is from a very close relative (mother, father, brother, sister) or school friend. They feel happy about the experience and want to share it, but when those around them are grieving, they may not do so because they feel guilty about feeling happy.

Very young children may wish to draw or paint what they have experienced. Again, it is very important to listen to them and let them share their experiences. Thankfully, more information is available to people nowadays. I still receive a lot of post from people who experienced contact from deceased loved ones when they were children. Many years later they are often still scarred by being told they were 'lying', 'mistaken' or 'making it up'. Worse still are the cases of those who were taken for psychiatric evaluation as a result of their visit from Grandma! Their experiences of afterlife contact were joyous and healing – the reactions of the adults around them were not!

As adults, these people are relieved to be able to talk to others on the Internet and read about people who have had similar events in their lives. This story came through my 'psychic children' forum on the Internet:

A message from heaven

My sister's five-year-old son said to his mother, 'Mom, didn't you say Gram Ruby was in heaven?'

The question came totally out of the blue, but my sister confirmed, 'Yes.'

Her son continued, 'Well, she says she loves you and she misses you!'

Our grandmother died when my nephew was two years old, he has no memory of her and my sister had not been speaking of her to him or anyone else recently. She lives about eight hours from the rest of our family so there is no one else he could have picked up this strange comment from.

Then five days later my sister was cooking dinner and her son was sitting at the table with her. He told her, 'Mom, Gram Ruby told me she left too soon. She wanted to see her birthday first...'

My sister rang my father to find out the actual date of death and Ruby's birthday. She had died on 10 April and her birthday was 19 May, so it's true, she didn't live to see her birthday!

'No one believes me'

Referring back to the problem of not being believed, it isn't something that is specific to children. Adults, too, can be faced with this lack of understanding. Religious and cultural beliefs can sometimes get in the way. No one is to blame as such, but not being believed is hurtful and confusing.

Luckily, as I've said before, there are now books and Internet chat rooms which will fill in the gaps when living friends and relations are unable to help or support you.

CHAPTER 6

Do Animals Have a Soul?

You think dogs will not be in heaven? I tell you,
they will be there long before any of us.

ROBERT STEVENSON

I receive many stories where deceased animals have visited their human owners after death, so I would have to say that I believe that animals do have a soul. This soul appears to continue after physical death and our pets are allocated their own corner of heaven. The loss of a pet is a devastating blow and it would be wrong not to include some information about this special kind of loss here.

GRIEVING FOR PETS

Pets become family members (and as I say this, right on cue my little black kitten sticks his head through the cat door). They are with us every day. They don't argue with us, they listen to our problems and then sit beside us when we're sad and lonely.

Our animals learn their own special tricks. Birds talk, cats purr and dog wag their tails. Their love is unconditional and it's only natural that their death brings a wide chasm into which we can fall. The loss is powerful and overwhelming, and for many people who live alone, the death of their daily companion is even worse than the loss of a human life. Also, people who are grieving for human friends will often find that the loss of a pet can bring back the pain of the human deaths all over again.

The understanding of our fellow human beings is not always available when it comes to the mourning of loving pets. People may not understand when we have to take a few days off work. 'It's only a dog,' they'll say. Yet the grief can be the same as for any other loved one, or even worse.

When ill pets have to be euthanized we have the added burden of guilt – that awful word again. Whether we choose to have our pets put to sleep or the decision is taken out of our hands by our local vet makes no difference to how we feel. People have said to me that they feel like 'murderers' because they have had to have a pet put to sleep, and having been through this experience myself, I totally understand.

ANIMAL SIGNS FROM THE OTHER SIDE

The need for a sign that our pets continue to exist in some

form is strong and they do seem capable of letting us know that they have arrived safely in their new heavenly home.

For many years I have been receiving post from pet owners. They feel their dogs curl around their legs and they waken to their cats making forbidden 'nests' on the bed, and all this happens *after* the death of the animals.

Pets, like our deceased human friends, can also appear in dreams and visions. Their goal is the same as that of the human visitors: to let us know that they are OK.

I've had dreams of my own pets, particularly of my dog Lady, who once appeared in a dream visitation surrounded by all of the other dogs we'd lost in the family over the years. If dogs could smile, then I'd have said she was doing it. Although she didn't speak to me using her mouth to form the words, I got a sense of her meaning. She told me, 'I'm here, I'm safe and I'm happy – and look, I'm with my friends.'

This visitation was of great comfort to me because I had felt guilty about Lady's death. Deep in my heart I knew it was her time and I had actually asked the vet to gently end her life rather than prolong her suffering, but I still wanted her to forgive me. Many people write to me with this same unnecessary request. The loving bond which exists between animals and their human owners continues after death and there is no need for guilt or forgiveness if you have acted out of love.

WHERE DO THEY GO?

It's hard to say with any certainty where our pets go when they pass over, but our spiritual friends have given us plenty of clues! I've spent many years investigating the phenomenon and this is what I've discovered:

- At the moment of death (and sometimes just before) the souls of our pets leave their physical body. They are drawn along on a sort of 'slipstream' that takes them to their final destination. It works like a sort of magnetic attraction and there is no chance that they will get lost along the way. Imagine a leaf floating along on the current of a stream.

- If our pets were in pain before they died, then this ceases the moment their spirits leave their physical body. The body is what carries the physical pain, not the soul. So all suffering ends at the time of physical death.

- Our pets can be with other animals, especially other family pets who have died (their friends!), or they might find themselves with others of the same species.

- Human souls who cared greatly for animals in life also care for animals in death and will watch over them as guardians. The animals themselves seem to be able to communicate with each other, with their human keepers and with us when they visit us.

- If we wish it, when we pass over, it is possible to create a space where we can reunite with our pets, on a permanent basis if we wish, or we can visit them if we choose.

- Although pets' personalities remain similar after death to in life, there is also a higher intelligence which accompanies their earthly visits and is presumably part of their new existence.

- Because our pets shed their physical bodies on death, food is no longer necessary. Species that might have seen each other as food in life can now co-exist safely.

******

WHAT DO THEY LOOK LIKE AFTER THEY DIE?

Like human souls, our pets usually show themselves to us as younger and healthier than they were at death. So if they appear to us visually, perhaps in a dream experience, dogs can look like puppies, cats might appear as kittens and horses might look like foals. Although strictly speaking their bodies are no longer necessary for their existence (they can now exist as a light energy, the pure soul), they can hold the form of the body they once owned if they wish. It's a personal choice on behalf of the soul (with a little help from the spiritual helpers).

By appearing so young and 'vibrant' – a word which many people use in their descriptions of their visiting pets – they are showing us how well they are, how healthy and happy.

Sometimes the pet is escorted by a 'minder' and at other times it is brought by a human relative on the other side. Here is one of many examples I have received – a visit by two lovely friends! This story comes from Scotland.

Reunited

My gran died in 1998 from heart disease. It was very sudden and totally unexpected. She was my father's mum and had lived with the family since the day I was born.

On the morning of the funeral I was drying my hair and crying at the same time, and all of a sudden the hair dryer went off by itself for about a minute then came back on again, which was strange.

Two weeks later, I was in my flat on my own. It was a Saturday morning about 9.30 and my boyfriend had just gone to work. I was just drifting back off to sleep when I heard the front door open again and I thought my boyfriend had forgotten something. The flat had a long hallway and I could hear footsteps coming up the hall. The next thing I felt was my bed sinking down as though there was somebody sitting next to me. I was stunned when I heard my gran begin to speak. I just couldn't open my eyes. Even though I tried hard to see her, I couldn't.

Gran told me she was fine and I laughed because she began to nag me about some dishes I had left in the sink.

We used to own the most beautiful dog and he had died three years previously. All of a sudden, there he was, jumping on me and licking my face. I kept pushing him back with my hands and my nana shouted at him to get off the bed. Then she went into the kitchen and I could hear her washing the dishes, even though I still couldn't open my eyes. I had to physically roll myself off the bed to wake myself up and by then she had gone. The really sad thing was that no one believed me afterwards, but I know it was real.

As with human souls, it is sometimes possible to touch the energy of a lost pet. They feel much the same as they did in life. It does take a lot of effort to create this special experience for us. Here is a great example:

Goodbye ... and hello again!

A year ago my dog Sasha became ill and I knew that her time to leave the Earth was close. She had been at the vet's for a few days and it was clear that her kidneys were failing her. She was a 12-year-old springer spaniel and still very beautiful to look at, but not the happy crazy little dog that she used to be.

My mam wanted to bring her home for a last weekend with the family, but unfortunately I was going away for the weekend so said my goodbyes to her before I left. I sat with her at the bottom of my parents' garden; tears were streaming down my face as I stroked her shaggy ears whilst she nuzzled into me. I whispered to her that when the angels came for her it was OK to go with them and I let her know it would be OK because she had looked after us long enough. I also told her that she could come back and lie on the bed and keep my feet warm any time she liked. It was one of the hardest things I have ever had to do.

The following day I phoned my mam to see how she was and as expected she was no better. A few hours later I was in Tesco's and my partner was dashing all over the place. All of a sudden I panicked and needed to get out of the shop. We left quickly and getting back into the car I saw I had missed a telephone call on my mobile phone. It had been my brother. I sent him a message telling him I couldn't call him back because I just knew what he was going to say... It took a while to open the message he sent back. As I had thought, he told me that our beautiful and faithful friend had died.

The following night, I dreamed that someone came to get me. I can't recall seeing their face, or seeing them at all, but I was taken somewhere where three tall figures in long black robes were standing together. Then they moved apart and there was our dog Sasha, just lying at their feet.

I didn't see the faces of the figures, but I remember cuddling Sasha and she felt so real. I could feel her fur and even smell her. I was crying in my dream and when I awoke I was cuddling the duvet. I felt so much better that day and then one night when I was curled up in bed reading I stretched out my legs and the bottom of the bed was warm... I just smiled.

In this next story, a dog's owner and her twin, who live in America, both had paranormal experiences relating to the loss of the pet:

Safe with the angels

Over a year ago my twin sister's five-year-old Pekinese mix called Bandit became ill all of a sudden. He was misdiagnosed with a slipped disc, but after three months of veterinarian visits he took a turn for the worse.

Two nights before he died, a young angel came to me in the middle of the night. I woke up and sat up in bed and saw her coming towards me in a white light. I'll always remember that she had dark hair, a white robe on and a large smile on her face. As I spoke to her, she turned and passed through the wall beside me.

It was so real that I told my sister about it. I'd never had anything like this happen to me before. At the time Bandit was at the vet's for emergency tests, so we were almost expecting the worst.

The next day Bandit was to have more tests and we went to see him before his operation. He already looked different. There was something in his eyes and he walked in a funny way. He just cried on my sister's shoulder and when we went to leave he cried again. I had to walk into the back to talk to the lady on the desk and I could still hear him crying. It was awful. He came through the tests, but just two days later, on Valentine's Day, Bandit lost his life. We found out later he had a disease with no cure.

Then a few weeks after he died Bandit visited my sister. She had an out-of-body experience and found herself in a white room. Bandit was right beside her. He appeared young again and was healthy and happy. She told him that she loved him and to be happy and

*he ran to a white bowl, drank and then ran off.
My sister told me that the experience was definitely
real.*

*After that we had lots of experiences. We could feel him
lying at our feet at night. Once my sister heard him
bark, then after a month my son and daughter and I
all saw him walk past our patio at home. My own dog
Scarlette (Bandit's sister) barked and I looked up and
there he was, bouncing across the patio! In fact he hung
around for quite a while.*

Animals often appear after a person has passed over.
They act in unusual ways to indicate that this is not a
'normal' animal appearance. Although I'm not sure that
our loved ones become the animal exactly, I feel that part
of their soul merges briefly with the animal so that it can
be a message-bringer.

This story really caught my eye:

The cat gatecrasher

*A strange cat decided to gatecrash my mother's funeral.
It waited outside with the congregation then came in
during the service. Friends tried to stop it to no avail.
It walked down the aisle, stopping to see who was in
each row, and then dived under the curtain to where
my mother's coffin was. As the vicar was saying the last*

prayer, it started crying at the top of its voice. Unbeknown to us, it had tried to climb on top of the coffin and fallen off.

A crematorium worker chased it out of the back door, but as we left the building it appeared again at the front! It came straight over to us whilst we were looking at the flowers and hung round my father's legs. My son and I started stroking it.

We eventually left, but were told later that the cat had hung around till the next day, when my mother's ashes were buried, then disappeared, never to be seen again.

I had asked my mother for a sign just to let us know that she was still around and asked if I could touch her or see her one more time. I think this was her reply.

CHAPTER 7

Goodbye Stories

I am ready to meet my Maker. Whether my
Maker is ready for the ordeal of meeting me
is another matter.

WINSTON CHURCHILL,
ex-British Prime Minister, on his 75th birthday

I love that quote. As we've already seen, Winston Churchill
had an interest in all things paranormal, and he wasn't the
only one. In a later chapter you will be stunned by the
famous figures whose lives have been touched by afterlife
phenomena!

OK, so what shall we look at next on our journey?
Amazing stories of spontaneous afterlife contact reach me
every day. It brings me great pleasure to share some of these
with you. Sometimes a simple story will illustrate so much
more than I can teach you in pages and pages of explanation.

These particular stories have been grouped together because they illustrate how souls come to collect our loved ones, how occasionally we can be warned of a passing and how our beloved relatives and friends come back to say goodbye once they've arrived safely in heaven.

Many souls seem to know that it is nearly time for them to leave. They just get a sense of it. Was this the case with Michelle's brother? I think it might have been.

Did he know?

My brother died two years ago, aged just 31, of a massive heart attack. He didn't know he had heart problems and I know this because I spoke to his doctor after he passed. He and I were very close and apparently he put me on a pedestal. He seemed to love me more than anything.

The night before he died he phoned me at 3.09 a.m. Obviously I was asleep, and he wouldn't normally have rung at that time unless it was an emergency. He said he just had to get a message to me. He was a bit drunk, as he had a drink problem most of the time. I spoke to him and he said he wanted to tell me that he loved me. He kept saying it and said I was his sister, his mum, his everything. He also said he appreciated everything I had done for him. He even thanked me for the birthday cake I'd made him when I was 12, for goodness sake!

I remember I burnt it and at the time I was very upset about it.

He never said anything about feeling unwell when he rang, but then he would never say anything which would worry me. To be honest, at the time I felt that the call was the sort of thing you'd make if you were going to take your own life, and I remember telling him not to do anything silly. He said, 'Don't be stupid.'

After a while I told him to go to bed and to call me in the morning to let me know he was all right. The next morning I rang him as soon as I got up. I remember it was around 9 o'clock. I called and called, but there was no answer. I was worried and when I spoke to his best mate he was concerned too. In the early hours of the following morning we decided to telephone the police. They responded immediately and made a forced entry into his house. They found him dead in bed. He was fully clothed. At first, because of my phone call, they thought he had committed suicide, but after a post mortem they found he had died of a massive heart attack.

Michelle wrote to ask me if I felt that her brother had expected to die. He seemed to show every indication that he felt his time was up. One wonders if he had experienced some sort of physical warning or maybe something spiritual had occurred to indicate that it was his time to leave. Of course, sadly we will never know, but this story is not unique. Our loved ones often seem to know when their time is close.

Here is an unusual 'announcing' and goodbye dream from Lori in Canada. It also includes some of the signs we talked about earlier in the book.

How would it be...?

My mother passed away nearly eight years ago. I was the eldest of four girls and occupied that special place in a mother's heart reserved for the first child. She died in her sleep of a heart attack. For a week before this I had been having a bad dream every night which I could not remember when I woke up, which was odd, as I usually remember my dreams. I put it down to the stress of starting a new job.

On the final night of the dream, I heard a voice ask how I would be if my mother died. In the dream, I replied that it would be difficult, but I would go on.

The next day, I went about my business as usual. I was ironing some clothes for work when I heard the same voice ask how long my mother's life would be. I stopped what I was doing and actually said out loud, 'Well, she's 71 now...' then shook away the thought as I went about my day. It turned out that she had been dead for a few hours at the time I was ironing.

Over the years, my mother has usually signalled to me in dreams that she is still with me. Recently, as I agonized over some changes I wanted to make in my life, she made it clear that she was still around.

I have cats and in the summer I get up very early and lock the sliding glass door open so that they can go in and out. On the anniversary of my mother's death (14 June) I got up at 5.30 a.m. and opened the door as usual. For some reason, I did not lock it open. I remembered this about half an hour later and got up to shut it, only to find it already shut. Like all mothers, mine was always concerned about household safety, so I felt that she had helped me out that day.

One day I could not find my make-up mirror, which always sits on my bedroom windowsill. Eventually I bought another one. A month later, I was doing some house chores and found the missing mirror under the bed. This was unmistakably my mother's work as, amusingly, she disliked vain women.

A couple of months ago, I was in high anxiety about whether or not to apply for a job that had opened up in my workplace. I applied, then held my breath for a week after the interview, waiting for word. One morning I could not find the jade pendant I always wear. Every night I place it, dangling on its chain, in the same spot.

The chain was there, but the pendant was gone. I was horrified, as this pendant had been a wedding gift to my mother from her mother and had deep sentimental value for me. I tore the house apart looking for it; I searched everywhere at work. For 24 hours I felt awful about it. I e-mailed a good friend who had just lost her mother and told her. She said that I would find it behind some furniture where I least suspected it to be. With that, I went to my bedroom and moved my big pine dresser out from the wall, and there was the pendant, dead centre, propped up against the wall!

If Mom had moved anything else, I might not have understood right away. In her way, she was shouting at me that she was with me and that things would be all right. I got the job, and the higher wages have meant fewer worries for me.

Just over a year after my mother died, my husband of five years passed away. I've had many visitations from him too. I really believe that his purpose in my life was to see me over the loss of my mother. I know that she would have been very upset to see me go through his loss too.

This next story is about a lady who was able to pick up information from her own angels, who gave her the information she needed to be with her father in his last hours.

'Each to its season'

My 88-year-old father was suffering from kidney failure and the doctors had told us they could only make him comfortable and the outcome was inevitable: he was just weeks away from dying. I asked my guardian angel how long he would suffer and first he showed me an egg-timer in my mind. I saw the sands running swiftly out. I asked for a clearer sign and was shown a large oak tree with golden leaves drifting down to the floor. When I asked what it meant, I heard the words: 'Each to its season.'

I understood the message, but being human I wanted a clearer sign: a date and a time. Was it possible? Then I heard what I had needed: my angel told me, '19 November at 11.08.' This was only a matter of days away. The nursing home was still telling us they would do blood tests on my father in a few weeks' time to see what was happening, but I knew that they would never happen. I trusted my inner voice.

I told my sister about the experience and shared the date with her. We both made sure we were at the home that day before 11.07 a.m., but I felt my father would pass during the evening.

During the day, Dad slept deeply. I could feel people around his bedside and knew that family members were waiting for him. My sister and I went home around teatime, but neither of us could settle. We just kept watching the clock as the evening progressed. At around 9.30 p.m. I decided to go back to the nursing home. My sister, who was at her own house 10 miles away, had also decided to drive back there. Moments later she got a call from the nurse in charge to say that Dad's temperature had shot up. She was immediately alerted, but the nurse assured her that Dad wasn't dying. She said it was up to us if we wanted to be with him or not. Of course we went. I packed up my bag with relaxing music and we both agreed no tears. This was Dad's time.

Dad's breathing was very shallow when we arrived. We dimmed the light and sat down next to him, playing the music for him. We talked to him and told him how much he was loved and what a good husband and father he had been. We reassured him that we would take care of Mum. Dad tried to reply, but sadly his message was unclear.

The staff told us at this point that he had pneumonia now as well. I remember asking the nurse if he could have something to help with his breathing and we were told they would visit in the morning to give him pain relief. I knew the morning would be too late, but they wouldn't listen.

Dad's breathing was bad. It was really slow now and both my sister and I noticed the time on the clock in the room was 11.10pm, two minutes after the time I'd been told. We told Dad it was his time to go and to just relax and leave this family and go to his 'old' family. His breaths gradually became fewer and fewer and then finally stopped altogether. He'd gone. The time was 11.37 p.m.

Being prepared made such a difference to my sister and me. It was such a privilege to be with Dad and comfort him as he left his physical body.

The next day we had to tell my 89-year-old mum (who was in the same home) that Dad had gone. We could hear her talking to someone, but couldn't see who it was. 'I'm chatting to the dog,' she said. She told us a man had brought it in to keep her company, but we couldn't see it! We often wondered if Dad had arranged for her to see the old dog they'd lost many years ago, to bring her comfort.

In life our visitors bring flowers, chocolate and even bottles of wine when they visit. It's customary to bring a special gift. This next man didn't forget in this special collection story.

Granddad collects Grandma – with flowers

I was in my thirties when I received a call to go to the General Hospital in Nottingham as my gran was very poorly. As I got to the side of the bed she looked at me, but then glanced over my left shoulder. The look of absolute delight that appeared on her face stopped me in my tracks! I was stunned when she then pointed up and beyond me and said, 'Why, here's Granddad coming with some beautiful flowers!' My granddad had physically passed the year before.

Now I understand that he was coming to collect her and take her 'over' to the other side, because she died later that night. I'll never forget that day.

As we've seen earlier, guilt, even when unnecessary, can hold a person back from carrying on with their life. So many people want to know if their loved ones forgive them. Granny Spivey wanted to bring reassurance from the other side. Here is Cindy's comforting story:

'It's OK, Cindy'

Last December my grandmother passed away. She'd been living in a nursing home and it was so hard for me when she died. On the day she was buried I decided not to go to the funeral. I said, 'Granny, forgive me for not going,' then I turned over to go to sleep.

I dreamed that I was lying on the bed and watching a shadow coming toward my side of the bed. I was frightened and asked it to stay away, but it kept coming towards me. I pulled the covers over my head, but then, as plain as day, as if I were seeing through the covers, the shadow became a human being and a voice said, 'It's OK, Cindy. It's me, Granny Spivey!'

I froze and then slowly opened my eyes to see my grandmother standing right over me. She took my arm and seemed to be trying to soothe me by saying, 'It's OK,' again, and then she said, 'I just came to say goodbye,' and she bent over and gave me a kiss on the cheek before she disappeared. It was so fast.

Then I woke from the dream and sat up on the bed with tears in my eyes. I swear it felt as though someone was still holding my arm and it stayed like that for quite a few minutes.

I have had many people tell me it was Granny's way of telling me it was OK that I hadn't gone to the funeral and that she understood and so came to me to say goodbye.

What is particularly great in this story is that people around Cindy were supportive of the experience.

As already mentioned, sometimes in a dream visitation we can physically touch our loved ones. Not every spirit can hold their energy together if we try and touch them, but I've read many accounts where visiting souls have been able to let us hug and kiss them and even hold their hands for several moments at a time. In most cases the hug is followed by the person waking up. Not in the following case, though.

A dream goodbye

I lost my youngest brother Richard last January. He was 23. We were extremely close and I felt as though part of me went with him. In the weeks after his death I was heartbroken. I prayed for him to let me know he was OK and told him repeatedly how much I loved him. I had always told him this when he was alive and although he never said it back (unless he'd been drinking), I knew he loved me too.

One night a couple of weeks after his funeral I had a dream, only it was different from any dream I'd ever had before. I remembered every detail and it felt as if everything in it was real.

In the dream I opened a door and could see into a room where Richard was standing. He was dressed in the clothes we cremated him in and I ran over to him and threw my arms round him! I was overjoyed and said to him, 'You're back, Rich! You can come home with me!'

He gently told me that he wasn't back and that he'd just come to tell me it was 'his time' and he had to go. He actually told me that he loved me very much and would always be with me. Then he put his arms round me...

I heard the door open and when I turned round it was ajar and when I turned back to Rich he was gone. It was this point that I woke up crying. I honestly believe that my brother had come to me to tell me he was OK and to say he loved me.

Since then I've had lots of little signs from him, mostly electrical, and each time something happens I say, 'Thanks, Rich, I know it's you!'

If you have a visitation experience of your own, remember to say thank you too. If our loved ones realize we are aware of their efforts they will know what to do next time to get a message through to us.

Remember that we also talked about loved ones coming back to see us when we felt we missed out on the opportunity to say goodbye? Here is a story which illustrates this type of visitation. It comes from Australia.

Goodbye on a bench

I was only 15 when my dad passed away unexpectedly. My parents had split up when I was small, but I still got to visit Dad every fortnight in the city. He didn't have a lot of money, but he always made sure that we had fun.

I remember the day he died. Mum and I had gone to his house and his flatmate had said he had been rushed to hospital the night before. Mum and I went to the hospital and tried hard to find him, but by the time we got there it was too late. I was devastated. We'd missed him by 20 minutes.

I cried for a long time after he died and always felt that I'd never had the opportunity to say goodbye.

A few years later I had a dream that my dad and I were sitting on a park bench, surrounded by whiteness. I could hear his voice so clearly, although I don't recall much of what we actually spoke about. I do remember him talking about my boyfriend Paul and telling me that he would be good to me.

I'd never heard of a dream visitation at that time, but it always felt very real to me and gave me the opportunity to say goodbye in the way that I'd missed at the time of his death.

Every now and then I still hear Dad's voice saying my name and I can see him in my mind smiling at me. I know he is still looking after me. I think he likes to spook my boyfriend, because I have a photograph in a frame of the two grandchildren my Dad never met and this particular photograph always falls forward!

We talked about photographs before and how people write and tell me that when they ask for a sign, their loved ones' photographs literally fall off the wall! Priceless!

As well as giving you the opportunity to say goodbye to a loved one, visitation dreams can warn you that it is someone's time. Rather than be sad when these warning dreams occur, try and see them as a real blessing. Here is as typical example of a warning dream where a loved one who has previously passed pops back to take another relative home. I always imagine the wonderful welcome-home party they must have.

Warning: It's time

During the evening of New Year's Day I had an extraordinary dreamlike visit from my dear dad, who'd passed away three years before. Sadly, it soon became apparent that Dad had come to warn me that he was coming to collect my uncle.

My poor uncle had only found out that he had cancer in November and it just seemed way too soon for him to die. I begged Dad not to take him, but it was his time and Dad just seemed to vanish away in front of me.

On the Tuesday I had a call at work. My sister was ringing to tell me my Uncle Jimmy had passed that day. I was still shocked, of course, but I only cried on the day of the funeral. I did feel a sense of calm that I had never had when my dad had died.

Do our loved ones have regrets about things they did and didn't do in life? Yes, they do. I have many experiences where a deceased loved one pops back to say sorry or, as in this case, just gets through to make sure someone hears the words that were unsaid, though very much meant, in life.

This story comes from England.

'He did love you'

Tom was my soul mate. I'd been through a traumatic time and he'd been there to comfort me and give me a shoulder to cry on. My feelings for him were true love, but although I knew he was very fond of me, he never actually told me that he loved me. Few knew about our relationship. We considered it a personal and private connection.

Tom was a bit of a bike fanatic. His Sundays were spent out on his bike enjoying the speed and the freedom of the road. He was a careful and cautious rider, but one Sunday he had a fatal accident. He collided with a car that had pulled out of a side road and died from his injuries two hours later in hospital.

There were lots of little coincidences after he died. Well, at first I thought they were just coincidences, but now I'm not so sure. The first sign came at the time of his accident. I'd been in the beer garden of the local pub and as we were leaving my friend asked if Tom was at the pub. 'No,' I said, 'he'll be out on his bike as it's such a lovely day.' Then for some reason I thought to myself, 'I hope he's OK.' I found out later that the time I was having that conversation was the time Tom had his accident.

Later that night I was at home waiting for Tom's usual Sunday evening text message and at the time he usually texted me sure enough I got one. Sadly, it wasn't from Tom but from a friend, who was unaware of my relationship with Tom. He'd contacted me to inform me of his death. As you can imagine, I was devastated! Was that his way of letting me know, I wondered?

The next sign came on the day of his funeral. I was taking my children to school and my car cut out several times. Up until that day I had never had the slightest problem with it. No lights were showing up on the dash to indicate there was a problem. When I got home I just sat at the wheel, put my head in my hands and cried, 'Don't you want me to make it to your funeral, Tom?'

Suddenly a thought came to me, 'Check the oil, check the oil.' Sure enough, when I checked the oil the dipstick was almost dry! If my car hadn't have kept stalling first thing in the morning I wouldn't have checked the oil and maybe wouldn't have made it to the funeral.

Weeks after Tom's funeral I was out one evening talking to some of his friends when a friend of his I hadn't spoken to before came over to me. He asked if I was Janet and I said yes. He said he'd been wondering how

I had been coping and that he had been looking out for me at Tom's funeral. He told me Tom had spoken to him about me and that he had told him that I was such a special person to him and that he loved me.

I can't tell you how wonderful it was to hear this. These were the magical words I'd waited to hear. Again, I wondered if maybe Tom had prompted his friend in some way to let me know.

There have been several times since when I have turned the radio on in my car and Tom's favourite artist, Paul Weller, has come on, or a song that reminds me of Tom has begun playing.

The last I saw Tom, he came to me in a dream. I was sitting round a table chatting and laughing with some friends when I felt I was being watched. When I looked up, Tom was standing by the table looking and smiling at me, but as I looked up he walked away. It was wonderful to see him.

My love for Tom is still very strong. I miss him terribly and think about him every day, but it's a comfort to know that he is still thinking of me from his new home.

This next goodbye story is from Sasha in India.

A goodbye sign

My grandfather was paralysed for about ten years before his death and by the end he was bedridden. First he stopped walking, then eating and after that he stopped talking. Sometimes he would say a word or two, but that was all.

We lived in different cities and when I visited him he would sometimes say my name and sometimes just stare into space. In the end he had to be fed through tubes. I always felt that there was a special attachment between us and it was hard to see him suffering.

Eventually he fell very ill and was admitted to the hospital and kept on a ventilator. The whole family was called because they thought it was his time. My parents went in first and then my brother and I visited the next day, but we were too late, because Grandfather passed away before we got to him.

I felt really bad that I didn't even get to see him before he passed on, but my dad hadn't had the chance to say goodbye either, because my grandfather had been unconscious when he'd seen him.

We came back to Bombay, where we were living, after a few days. Hindus perform a Pooja – a special ceremony – on the thirteenth day after the death and on that day my parents went to Delhi to perform the ceremony along with the rest of the family.

That morning I dreamed of my grandfather. I saw that he was in hospital and he was sick and I was asking him to hold on for a little longer, but he said no, it was time to go and he couldn't stay any longer.

So then I thought that maybe it was time and I had to let him go. In my dream I asked him if he would wait until my dad came because I knew he wanted to say goodbye too. Just then my dad entered the hospital room and my grandfather passed on.

I still feel this might not have been an ordinary dream. They say the spirit leaves the Earth on the thirteenth day of death, which is why we have the ceremony then. I think my grandfather came to say goodbye to me because when I was at his cremation I was so grief-stricken and so furious at the same time that I kept telling him in my head, 'You didn't even wait until I came to see you...' I think this was his way of saying goodbye before he finally left.

This next story is from Australia. I am sure that it is difficult for our loved ones in the afterlife to judge how hard to touch us, to let us know that they are with us, while not frightening us in any way. I'm sure this dear dad didn't mean to slap quite so hard!

A coffee smell

My dad was dying from cancer and we spent his last day with him. After he had passed, we left the hospital room and tried to deal with what just happened. You just can't think of anything at all and we all went home feeling bereft.

The next morning I came downstairs to make coffee and all I could smell was the room in the hospital. It was very strong. As I was grieving, I was unaware that it was Dad trying to let us know he was with us. The smell remained for most of the day.

After his funeral Dad came to me in a dream and showed me he was with my mother and they were lying in a hammock. This was very strange, as were the clothes they where wearing, so I have no idea why he showed me that!

Three days later he smacked my arm three times and woke me up. I wondered why he did that! He was a loving father who was very close to me and I feel him around me a lot.

My son has noticed the 'room smell' also and he was amazed by how strong it was. He has also experienced strange whispers in his ear and gentle touches, and has dreams of my dad too. I haven't seen him, apart from in that dream, but I have felt his touch and I know he messes with our clocks too.

I believe Dad will be with us forever and that makes me feel good. I know he still loves us all dearly.

CHAPTER 8

Messages from Heaven

Blessed are those who mourn,
for they shall be comforted.

MATTHEW 5:4

I have received so many amazing stories of loving contact from the other side, it's been hard to decide what to leave out. I have tried to pick out a selection of different types of experience here to show you the extent of what spirits seem able to do.

I love stories like this first one where our loved ones appear in dreams to show us that they are following a similar pattern to one they followed in life.

'See you on Friday'

I had a dream visitation from my cousin about a week ago. Initially I dismissed it as just a dream, but then a friend of mine said to me, 'Julie, Martine is visiting you. She is contacting you!' Of course she was!

In my visitation, I went to visit my aunt (Martine's mother) at her home. She looked so much better – happier – than she had been since Martine passed away. In the dream I said to her, 'Anna, you look so much better. What's going on?' She replied, 'Martine's been visiting me!'

I was not shocked at this because I had been reading up on this type of thing on your website. I was about to ask her how she was being visited when my cousin walked through the front door, right in front of my eyes! It was so vivid, much more so than just an ordinary dream. We greeted one another and I was so happy to see her and I asked her how she was and what it was like on the other side. She told me that she was doing great, she was so happy and told me that it was absolutely wonderful where she was. Then she turned around, walked back out the front door, waved and said, 'I have to go now. Bye. Bye, Mom, I'll see you on Friday.'

When I woke up, the dream was very clear to me and I could recall everything in detail. In ordinary dreams things seem a bit hazy and I cannot recall everything and sometimes nothing at all. I felt so happy after I woke up. I wasn't sad about my cousin having passed on at all. I guess you could say that I felt very comforted.

I decided not to tell my aunt straight away, as I did not want to upset her, but when I met up with her for coffee yesterday I decided to tell her. When I recounted that I saw Martine turn to wave goodbye, saying, 'Bye, Mom, I'll see you on Friday,' my aunt was amazed and asked me whether I knew that Martine used to visit her every *single Friday! I hadn't been aware of this and it gave me further confirmation that I really had had a visitation from Martine.*

I have to thank you again. If I hadn't read about your work, I don't believe I would have been open to receiving messages from my cousin. I would probably have dismissed both experiences as coincidences! Yet it's funny, later I remembered I'd also received a message from an old university friend who passed away about six years ago!

This has all brought me so much comfort and peace.

In this next story the dream experience is about a telephone call. These differ from normal dreams in that our thinking is rational in the way it would be in waking life (ordinary dreams are very muddled). I've had several similar experiences sent to me over the years, and, as we've already seen, to keep up with modern technology, sometimes the telephone is a mobile phone.

'It's me ... Mam'

I was very close to my mum, who suffered from epilepsy. As she was ill regularly I used to look after her and even when she was well I always worried about her and called her on the phone most days.

Even though she had been ill for a long time it was still a terrible shock when she died. In January she was found dead in her bed. (She always said she wanted to go this way.) The verdict was 'adult cot death'.

A week after she died, I had a vivid dream in which my telephone rang and my mum said, 'Hi, Pauline, it's me.' I was aware that she had died and wondered how anyone could be so cruel as to say this on the phone. I got cross and asked, 'Who is it?' All the while I was rationalizing that it couldn't really be my mum because she was dead!

Mum started laughing. She said, 'It's me ... Mam! I just want to let you know that I'm OK.' I asked her if she'd spoken to my brother and she said, 'No, not yet.'

The next scene unfolded in front of me and I was in my dining room looking at my brother hugging my mum and she was giggling because he was so happy. I remember feeling really happy too because my brother had had the chance to see her too. I was so convinced that she had contacted me through my dream that I asked my brother the next day if he'd had the dream too, but sadly he didn't remember it.

Although it's rare, I have heard of cases where two or more people *have* had the same dream on the same night because the deceased relative has been able to visit several people on one night. It would be more normal for the people to interact with the deceased one at a time and see other relatives maybe facing away and waiting their turn. On other occasions several relatives or friends are visited over the course of days or weeks.

Don't be offended if you are not visited and others are – sometimes there are 'technical difficulties' to do with psychic ability, suitable dream incubation, the ability or experience of the visiting spirit, what 'level' you dream on, timing and so on. It's nothing personal. Take each family visitation experience as a loving gift for everyone to share.

'Hello, Janet'

I had a strange experience last year when a friend's daughter, Janet, died totally unexpectedly. Twice that day I 'saw' her in town, and then realized that it wasn't her at all. On one of the occasions I was on my way to work at about 8.55 a.m. which is about the time Janet died. I was late for work and remember thinking, 'Oh no, there's Janet. I'll have to stop and talk to her and then I'll be really late for work!' Later that day I again thought I saw her, and remember thinking how odd it was to think I had seen Janet twice in one day, when normally I never saw or even thought much about her!

When a mutual friend rang me two days later to tell me of Janet's death, I was totally shocked and amazed. I was not particularly close to Janet, so cannot imagine why I should 'see' her twice on the day she died. I have not told my friend about this, in case she thinks I am 'peculiar'.

I've done something similar – you know when you see someone and it reminds you of a person you haven't seen for years and then you bump into that exact person in another place the following day or their name comes up in conversation. Weird, isn't it?

But our dream visitations don't have to be complicated in any way. Sometimes our loved ones appear very briefly.

This experience is from Wilhelmina in the Netherlands.

Angel in the light

A couple of years ago I woke up in the middle of the night and there was a beautiful light person. At first he stood at the end of the bed, at the side where my husband always sleeps, and then suddenly, before I could count to two, he was near my husband's sleeping body and looking over at me, and I saw the love in his eyes. He just looked at me, waved and was away.

A couple of days later he was there again. He was so beautiful and had this look of love again. Suddenly I was thinking about our daughter as well as wondering who this person was. She was just fine, though. Was the light being an angel, Jesus or one of my husband's two brothers who passed away many years ago? I have often wondered.

I know that my cat Daisy can see spirits, but I think many animals can.

Modern technology seems to feature more and more in the stories people send me, as in this example from England:

Computer, goodbye

My nephew tragically took his own life. He was always on his computer chatting to his friends on MSN Instant

Messenger. I had only recently bought a computer, so was just learning, but two days after his death I decided to go on MSN just to see who was online when out of the blue (and I know this is hard to believe) my nephew's photo popped up on the screen with the message 'Hello, Aunty Tina, I'm OK' and then went offline again!

The hairs stood up on my neck and I immediately rang his mother and asked if anyone was tampering with his computer. She said his computer was still in his flat and the police had boarded the place up while they conducted further enquiries.

When they eventually got into the flat they found the computer was on, just as he left it when he died.

I still can't believe it happened like this, but it's the truth. I miss him so much and I really do hope he is OK now.

We talked earlier about how bad we can feel when our relationships with our relatives are not as we would wish them to be. When we fall out with loved ones in life and then lose them, it's hard to move on. Visitation experiences are very helpful in healing, as this experience from Italy illustrates:

'I wish he didn't hate me'

I moved away from my family to train to be a teacher. One night I was getting ready to go out with friends when I received a phone call from my older sister to say that my younger brother Graeme had died. This was very sudden and there had been no illness or accident. He simply passed away in his sleep eight days after his 22nd birthday.

Since then I have felt a lot of guilt about my brother and the relationship we had. I had not spoken to him for several months before he passed, except for a few texts on his birthday. I took his death very badly and am still struggling to come to terms with things nearly three years later.

About six months after my brother's death I was driving my car and thinking about him. I said aloud, 'I wish I knew that you didn't hate me.'

I returned to the house I was sharing with some friends, but no one was home, so I went for a shower. In my room I have a CD player that holds three CDs. At the time, one of them was The Burt Bacharach Collection. *When I went into the shower, the CD player was off, but when I returned to my room, it was playing the song 'Magic Moments' that was used in the*

Quality Street adverts years ago. My brother used to love that song when he was younger. I took that to be the sign that I was looking for.

My sister's six-year-old daughter told her that Uncle Graeme had visited her too, while my mum and oldest sister keep seeing robins that seem to stand and stare at them for a while before flying off, and they take them to be a sign from him.

In this next story, I believe that this gentleman's ex-wife had reached out specifically to comfort him in his time of grief. This is another story from England.

Safe in the light

I wanted to share this with you, as it was an amazing experience. I was once married, but eventually we went our separate ways. She married again and I believe she had about three children.

One night I was organizing the music at a party when a lady came over to me and asked my name. I told her and she said, 'Oh, have you heard about your ex-wife?'

I replied, 'Has she had another baby?'

'Oh no,' she said. 'She is dead!'

I have had many shocks in my lifetime, but this was as if someone just reached into my stomach and ripped it out. I fell backwards and leaned up the wall for a while and just let the CD carry on playing. My ex-wife would only have been 31 at the time. I got through the party and went home and then I just climbed into bed and lay there with the quilt over my head.

Eventually I asked her to come and let me know she was fine and at peace. I asked her to slam the door, knock something off the shelf, anything at all, but just to contact me.

I was so upset and remember lying there with tears running down my face. I was certainly not expecting what came next. The room filled with light so bright it came through the quilt. I thought that maybe the security light had come on in the back garden, so sat up in bed. To my amazement there was a full figure of light standing at the end of my bed. I knew it was my ex-wife. The light was really bright, but it never hurt my eyes, and with it came a feeling of pure love.

I just sat on the bed and stared in amazement. 'Please don't go,' I said, but after about 30 seconds she faded away. I have never worried about her since then and I slept very well that night too.

Writing this is just another way of saying thank you to her again. Sometimes it is hard to tell people what you have seen, as they think you are crazy. It's a very personal thing to be touched by a relative from spirit. I only wish that more people could experience it. It's the best thing that has ever happened to me.

Here's another story that features the use of modern technology to bring signs. This man also made full use of the dream visitation experience to show himself clearly to his daughter, just in case there was any doubt that the messages were from him.

Hello in a mist

I lost my dad in May and was absolutely devastated. He had been diagnosed with cancer only eight weeks before he died and suffered tremendously, so in a way his passing was a relief, but it was also a massive loss to all of us.

During the week before his funeral all kinds of strange things were happening in my home. My TV was flicking through the channels on its own and my phone kept ringing all the time with no one at the other end. People tried to call me on my home phone and were getting through to other numbers.

I had a friend whom I had not spoken to for about six months prior to my father's death. She texted me the day after he died to ask if I was OK, as she had been getting text messages from my phone that didn't say anything but just showed my number. I have a pay-as-you-go phone and had no credit on it to be able to send anything!

My mother was absolutely devastated at the loss, but two months after my father's death she decided to take a few days' break in Portugal with a friend to just relax a little. She left for the airport at 3 a.m. and 20 minutes later that same night I was woken by the strange feeling that I wasn't alone. I saw a misty kind of figure, but it seemed to be very tall or floating above floor level. I didn't see my dad's features but I just knew it was him. I think he had come to see me as my mum had just left the house to go away and he was maybe wondering where she was going. I wasn't frightened at all, even though it was strange, because I had a feeling of peace and love, but also it made me feel extremely tired.

On another occasion shortly after my dad's death I had gone to spend an evening with friends and was staying overnight. I got into bed and was thinking about my dad and wondering what it felt like to be where he was. I remember wishing I could experience what it felt like to be in heaven.

I dropped off to sleep right away and I remember a feeling of absolute bliss, happiness and love. It was amazing. It didn't last long, maybe a few minutes, but it was like nothing I had ever experienced before. I always wondered if it was my dad showing me how heaven actually did feel.

In another dream I walked into a room alone and my dad was there, leaning on a table. I said, 'Dad, how lovely to see you, but I thought you had died?' He just smiled and didn't say anything, but when I woke up I felt very settled, as though I knew he was OK.

I feel him around me all the time and I'm sure I can feel someone touching my hair when I lie in bed at night (I live alone). I truly believe in an afterlife and after having these experiences I am even more convinced we move on to a better place.

It is possible to feel closer to someone after they have died than when they were alive? The afterlife communication experience seems to make up for lost time. Certainly I know this to be true with my own experiences. I have an uncle whom I got to know a lot better after he died. His visits in dreams really brought me closer to him. I know that my sisters, who are also aware of his presence, also feel the same way.

Here is story that has a similar theme:

Not scared since Grandma's visit

My grandmother died in December and as I was due to go away on holiday my parents didn't tell me of her death until I came back in the January, which was also when I was moving house.

Before I did so, I started having strange fears. At night-time I'd cover all the mirrors and close the curtains before it got dark, and I wouldn't get out of bed or go into another room without switching the light on because I was scared of seeing ghosts! Why these fears started I've no idea, but I do know they only started once I'd found out my grandmother had died.

Anyhow, I moved into my present house and I know for sure that my grandmother visited me there. In her house she had a pantry with a distinct smell. When I went into our downstairs toilet, which we also use as a pantry, I could smell that familiar scent.

I also started to dream about her a lot. The very last dream I remember is having a meal with her and then going to the cashpoint and taking out £20, which I gave to her, along with a big hug goodbye.

Funnily enough, we weren't close in real life, but I feel that we are closer now. I have a 'sixth sense' that she is around and pops in to say hello from time to time. By the way, since I moved into my present house I've had no fears about seeing ghosts!

I hope my story is of interest to you. It does show that spirits don't just appear as apparitions and do contact us in many different ways. I know if my grandmother had appeared to me in real life, I'd have run a mile!

Our loved ones can be very aware of what is going on in our lives and can be very comforting to us, even though they can be just there in the background. Reassurance dreams like this next story are quite common.

A reassuring visit

My husband of 33 years died of cancer in June and I've been trying to come to terms with it and get my life back together. I had booked flights to Spain to spend two weeks with friends who live there in the hope that I would be able to relax and wind down after everything I'd been through. Unfortunately I had to cut this to one week as something urgent cropped up which upset me extremely. Then four days before I was due to fly I found out that a serious allegation had been made against one of my sons, but nobody would discuss it with my other son and me. We were told we would have to wait until a meeting could be convened.

I couldn't go away without knowing what the allegation was and what would happen.

I sobbed my heart out two evenings in a row and eventually turned to my husband's photograph to ask him, 'Why is this happening to me?'

An unusual thing happened to me that night. I am rarely aware of my dreams, but that night was different. I had a dream that was so vivid it will stay with me forever. My husband began to appear in front of my eyes. I tried to touch him, but my hand went right through him as if he were made of mist. Slowly he became solid and he spoke to me, saying that he had been sent back to reassure me. I asked him how he had got back and he said he didn't know, but he was back.

He held and kissed me then and it felt as though I was in heaven. He sat down in an armchair and I said to my other son, 'Look, look, it's Dad,' but he just looked blankly at me as if I was insane, because he couldn't see him at all.

I was afraid to take my eyes off him in case he disappeared. He seemed to sit there for ages. He didn't say anything else but just smiled his lovely smile. Once I looked away and when I looked back the chair was empty and I was panicking that he had gone, but he had only moved to another chair. He stayed with me right until I woke up.

I felt much calmer after that experience and I knew that my husband was watching over me. Two days later, it turned out that the allegation was unfounded and I was able to go away with a great burden lifted from my shoulders. I felt that my husband had been trying to tell me that everything would be all right.

I often hear afterlife contact stories from people who've had a near-death experience. Many of those who come back from the point of physical death have seen loved ones, angels or spiritual guides who have sent them back to continue their earthly lives and live out their pre-life plans.

Nicola is from England and her deceased nan helped her back into her body when she had a near-death experience:

'It's not your time'

Ever since my son Liam was ten months old he's had contact with the afterlife. He is seven now and is autistic, but claims to have seen many spirits. My nan passed away suddenly when he was five, but he tells me that when he's asleep he goes to where she lives now.

When my nan was in hospital she fell and bruised her face and I have never mentioned it to Liam, but two weeks after she had passed over he came to me when I was crying in the kitchen and said, 'Don't cry, Mummy. Nanny Silv's face is better now.' When I asked how he knew, he said she had come to see him.

Then in September I went into hospital for open heart surgery. I've had many heart operations and have never been scared, but this time I knew something wasn't right. Before I went into theatre I said to my friend, 'What if I die?' She told me not to be so silly.

After my operation there were complications and I had to go back on bypass. My family was called to the hospital and the doctors told them I wasn't going to make it, but if by some remote chance I did, I would probably be brain-damaged. It must have been an awful shock.

I don't remember much about what happened, but I do recall hearing my partner ask me if I was 'OK, sweetheart' and it felt as though I was having a bad dream. Then I felt as though I was being chased and I called out to my nan and suddenly she was standing there in front of me. I walked towards her, but she pushed me away and as she did so I felt myself falling. Then I opened my eyes and I had pulled my tube out and didn't know where I was or what had happened.

My dad was standing by the bed and he explained that I had been asleep for a whole week. I don't recall going into hospital, but I do know what happened to me was real. My nan pushed me back because it wasn't my time, but it was lovely to see her again.

CHAPTER 9

Signs from Above

Has this world been so kind to you that you should leave with regret? There are better things ahead than any we leave behind.

C. S. LEWIS

We have already talked a little about the signs that our loved ones bring us to let us know that they are around us still. We need a 'little something' to show us that they hear us, see us and are still a part of our lives, or maybe just to let us know that they have arrived safely.

Here is a great example from my own life. My daughter started a new job today and she asked for a sign that everything was going to be OK. Less than a minute afterwards she felt something like a small stone landing on her head. She was sitting on the top deck of a double-decker bus at the time – and yes, it had a roof on! She told me she looked around on the floor, but could find nothing. She was convinced she had her sign. I'd also told her that her grandfather was going to work with her on her first day. I'm convinced he was with her and was giving her a very physical sign that he was there.

I thought it would be fun to gather just a few more of this type of story together for you here.

Although many signs come to calm and reassure us during our normal waking day, i.e. when we *ask* for a sign, as in the example above, they are more likely to come when we feel distressed or even depressed. Here is the story of a simple sign which came following a very sad time:

'Send me a sign'

My dad died three years ago and very tragically my mother died nine weeks later whilst I was in the USA attending my son's wedding. Although it was comforting to know they were together, the shock of the double loss was overwhelming at the time.

I'd always wanted to know if they were still around me and I thought I would ask them for a sign, although I had to say I was doubtful that anything would happen.

The next morning I was drying my hair in my bedroom and a picture of my dad which has been sitting above

my window for three years fell down in front of me!
I felt fairly confident that I'd received my sign.

There are many, many ways of receiving signs. I get a lot of signs surrounding butterflies – moths, too, but mainly butterflies. They are brilliant signs from the other side.

'Are white butterflies signs too?'

When my mum died we were all very shocked by the suddenness of her passing, even though she was 83 years old and had been ill on and off for some time. Unfortunately we were not informed that she was in hospital until the early hours of the morning, although she had been taken there at 8 o'clock the previous evening. When we got there she was unconscious and being kept alive by a ventilator. In my opinion she was already brain-dead and in fact she died later that day at 4 p.m.

My husband, brother and sister and I were all with her when she died, but none of us had had the chance to say goodbye to her while she was still conscious. I was terribly upset by this.

In early November, a few days after she died, I was sitting alone at home when I saw a plain white butterfly. I remember thinking that it was unusual to see a butterfly in the house at that time of year and wondered if it could be some sort of sign, but immediately dismissed the thought. I remember thinking to myself that if the butterfly had been brightly coloured, like a Red Admiral, it might have meant something, but a plain white butterfly seemed too ordinary.

Mum's funeral was held on 4 November. We went back to her house afterwards and I was talking to someone when I glanced up at the window and there, on the inside, was a large brightly coloured Red Admiral butterfly! I was amazed and somehow comforted, and went home afterwards and looked up Red Admiral butterflies to see what time of year they usually appeared. It would seem that it is very unusual to see one in November. This gave me comfort and helped me to come to terms with my mother's sudden death.

It's interesting how we try and explain away our experiences. 'If it were only *this* I would believe.' 'Perhaps if it had happened at *that* time it would have been real...' We often need more than one sign before we are sure.

This next story is one about a psychic smell.

White Musk

My lovely mum passed over after a very difficult time when she was suffering from Alzheimer's. For the last year of her life she was in a residential home and hated every minute of it, as I did. Even after three years I still cringe and get tearful when I think of her in there.

Eventually she got pneumonia and was in hospital for the last five weeks. The first day I was told she was going into hospital I left work and drove like a maniac from my home in Oxford to get to Manchester. When I got there she was having her blood pressure taken and was like a rag doll, with no life in her eyes whatsoever. When I walked in, her eyes took on life and she held my hand and said, 'Don't leave me.' I promised her I would never leave her again and I sat with her every single day and evening for those five weeks.

After her passing I returned to work. I am a senior prison officer. It is a male prison, so there's not an awful lot of perfume around! One day I was sitting in the office on the wing when one of my male colleagues walked in and said, 'Ooh, White Musk.' I got goose bumps immediately and asked why he had said that. He told me, 'I could smell it really strongly when I walked into the office, but it's gone now.' I told him that White Musk was my mum's favourite and I had never worn it. He said, 'I only know the smell because an aunt of mine used to wear it years ago.'

People often write and tell me that they believe a loved one is watching over them, and even that they have saved their life. Annette's story comes from Canada.

Dad to the rescue

It was a snowy winter's night and my husband and I were travelling with our friends to their camp. One friend was driving the pick-up truck and my husband was sitting in the front with him. Another friend and I were sitting on the back seat.

The highway was very narrow and windy and we were pulling a trailer with two snowmobiles on the back. There was no shoulder to pull over onto if you needed to stop.

On the journey I was talking about my father, who had passed away approximately nine months earlier. I'd had a bit of a hard time with his passing away and he had visited me twice in my dreams. The first time was just one week after his death and he had let me know that he was happy. I was fine after that because I knew that even though it was a dream, he really had visited me.

After our conversation about my father had ended, we realized we were in danger. Two sets of lights were right in front of us. We were on a curve going uphill and one vehicle, a truck, was in our lane and was passing a van coming in the other direction! We had nowhere to go and all I remember is screaming and closing my eyes...

The next thing I knew, we were still on the road and alive when we should have been dead! I couldn't believe what had just happened. How could we still be alive? There was no way on Earth we could fit three vehicles wide on that highway, especially two huge transporters and a truck!

Nobody spoke for what seemed like 15 minutes. I was the first to find my voice and asked my friend what he had done to avoid the accident. He swore he hadn't done anything because he hadn't had time to react. He just remembered having the feeling that he wasn't really there, as if he had missed a few seconds after we seen the lights in front of us. That's when the emotions surfaced for all of us, because we knew that my father had been with us during that time. There is no other explanation for what happened that night. We were saved by an angel!

It does seem more than a coincidence that this lady had been talking about her father one minute and had her life saved the next. He really was her angel that night. Did you notice the section where the driver suggested 'missing seconds'? The mysteriousness of this incident seriously suggests an 'otherworldly' experience to me!

This next lady wrote me a very long letter and I have included some of it here as she has had so many experiences. Nicole is from Holland.

Experiences from Holland

I'm a 37-year-old woman from Holland. When I was about 20 I was sitting in a bus and I heard someone call out my name. I had a Walkman on, so I took it off and looked around, but no one was looking in my direction. I put my Walkman back on, but I couldn't stop thinking about it. The moment I got home, I knew why I had heard it. My boyfriend's grandmother had died.

A while later I was blow-drying my hair when I heard someone calling my name again. I switched the hairdryer off and said, 'Yes?' My boyfriend came out of the kitchen and said, 'What?' I asked him if he had called me, but he hadn't. So I start thinking about it and said to myself, 'Remember this day.' It was just as well that I did that, because a few days later I heard that my father's cousin had died. My grandfather told me this and I immediately asked him when it had happened. When he told me, I was shocked. It was the very day and time that I had heard someone calling my name!

I have had this experience a few times more, but I can't remember the details now. It seems to me I only have it when there is a lot of noise around me, such as the Walkman and the hairdryer.

When I was pregnant with my younger son my grandfather died, but he came to me the week after his death and spoke to me in words that I knew could only come from him. It happened at the moment between being awake and asleep, the moment one is most open to these things.

Years later I tried to make contact with one of my spirit guides. One evening I asked my guide to make one part of my body really hot so I would know he was there. He did! I always have cold hands and my right hand started getting warmer and warmer! I felt so happy! I started talking to him and discovered he was from Teheran. Now I sometimes talk to him and sometimes he starts talking to me.

Two years ago my grandfather on my mother's side died. I was about to visit him, but I was too late. I was so angry with myself. But in the week before the funeral I heard my grandfather talking to my deceased mother about the life they had had together. In all the years since my mother had died I'd never heard her talking, though she'd appeared in my dreams twice. Some time later my aunt called me on the phone. She told me she'd seen my mother in a kind of dream. She said, 'She was standing in the hallway near my bedroom smiling at me. Then she waved and I knew she would go over to the other side.'

One morning my elder son told me my mother had been with him that night. I was amazed and wanted to know everything about it. He told me he hadn't seen her, but he had felt her. I asked him where and he said, 'Here!' pointing at his heart. He said, 'I could feel love right here and I knew it was Oma.' Immediately my younger son told me he had heard her telling him she loved him and had also felt the love. I immediately felt that was right, as she had been with me when he had been born and they had had a very strong bond.

Nicole continued to relate more experiences that her family had been through over the years. Many people write to me with one experience and then write back with more and more things that they remember. Wouldn't it be fun to start a scrapbook of family psychic and paranormal experiences? Imagine passing the book down through generations and sharing the experiences with family and friends.

We all have these bizarre 'That was strange, wasn't it?' moments. The more we acknowledge them by talking about them and writing them down or e-mailing them to other people, the more things happen to us. I really believe that our loved ones are waiting for us to say 'Oh, I got that message, thank you' so that they know it worked and they can send us more.

I love the different ways our loved ones reach us. They often mess with clocks. Many people have found their watch stops at the exact time that a loved one dies. The following story is another version of this experience.

A watch 'coincidence'

I recently found my husband's gold watch. I'd bought it for him as a birthday present a few years ago. He had to stop wearing it as he was allergic to the material. It had stopped a few years previously and when I looked at it, it read 'Sun. 3'. My husband died on a Sunday and the date was the 3rd.

Amy also had some wonderful signs from the other side:

Grandpa's visits after a family is reunited

In 1999 my parents divorced and subsequently I went to live with my father while my mother moved about an hour's drive away. I was 14 at the time and felt somewhat abandoned by my mother and chose not to have contact with her.

My mother lived in the same town as her parents, so seeing them was somewhat awkward. My grandpa was always a very fair and loving person and loved all of his grandchildren equally. Apparently he always said that he still loved me too, although he never fully understood my lack of contact with my mum.

Last May my stepfather asked me to go to my mother's birthday party at the beginning of June. I did attend and although it was somewhat strange at first I enjoyed it and kept in touch with my mum from then on. A few days after the party I rang her and asked why my grandparents hadn't attended and she said it was because my grandpa was too ill; he'd been in and out of hospital for a year or so.

I asked my mum if I could go and visit him. She relayed the message to him and he said it would be fine. But he died the next day, before I got to see him. Of course I went straight over and the nurses said that they would leave his body until I'd said my goodbyes.

I have never seen a dead body before and was somewhat apprehensive, but when I went into my grandpa's room I felt a sense of calm. It was strange; the body didn't look like my grandpa, but when I went to kiss his cheek I felt and heard what I can only describe as an intake of breath. (It was about four hours since he'd passed.) I was a little freaked out, but at the same time calm, as it was my grandpa.

I found out later that he had always said to my mum that he wouldn't go until I was a part of the family again. I believe that he passed the day after the conversation with my mum about my visit because he'd done his job and got his wish.

Since he died, I believe he has been to visit me in several different ways. A few weeks after the funeral I was sitting reading in the garden when all of a sudden the chair next to me moved as though someone had sat down on it. I immediately freaked out and ran inside to phone my mum. She told me not to be scared in case it was Grandpa and to go out there and ask him to come back. I did this and even asked out loud for him to visit me again. It took ages and I became desperate for him to come back, but eventually he sat in the chair again and he didn't leave until I'd finished reading and had to get up to go to work.

Later I had just finished university and was going through a rough patch both financially and personally. I'd just broken up with my partner and was having a lot of expensive problems with my car. I'd left my job at a pub because they had cut down my hours and I had started work somewhere that I didn't like and that paid less money. So I asked my grandpa out loud if he could help me again. I wanted him to make things easier for me, not to give me a complete solution, but within the next month I was back with my partner and I had a new car (with a loan at an unbelievably low interest rate). And the landlord of the pub had called me and asked me to come back to work for him. He even offered me full-time hours.

Was this just a coincidence or was it my grandpa? Maybe both, but I believe my grandpa was behind the 'coincidence'! I am happier now than I have ever been.

Don't leave it too long to reconcile with your own family. Remember the age-old saying (and song) 'Love is all there is.'

Amy also told me about a funny dream in which she felt her grandpa was telling her that he was lonely because no one spoke to him any more. On a hunch she rang her mother and asked her about the urn that held Grandpa's ashes. Her mother explained that it had been moved from the hallway where it was usually kept to the spare room. I assume that as people had walked through the hall they had remembered Grandpa and spoken to him, but they weren't doing it any more.

You don't have to keep an urn in your hallway to remember someone, though. A regular bunch of flowers in a vase, a framed photograph or perhaps a pretty box, picture or figurine can all remind you of someone you love.

Do talk to your loved ones from time to time. Speak to them as if they were still with you. They are.

CHAPTER 10

Celebrities and the Afterlife Experience

'People are like snowflakes – every one is special.'

ANON.

It's strange how people take notice of something that happens to people in the public eye. It's as if we somehow trust them more. 'Well, if it's happened to so-and-so then it must be real!' Of course the truth of the matter is that we are all human; we all suffer bereavement and grief and we all need reassurance that our loved ones are safe and well.

During my research I've come across a lot of afterlife stories involving famous people. I thought you might enjoy reading about some of them here.

Ingrid Bergman

Charlotte Chandler is the author of the book *Ingrid: Ingrid Bergman, A Personal Biography* (Simon & Schuster, 2007), which is based on conversations with the actress personally and with people who were part of her life, including her daughter Isabella Rosselini.

Ingrid was born in Sweden in 1915 and sadly her mother, Frieda Adler, died when she was a very young girl. Ingrid herself lived to the age of 67; she actually died on her own birthday. Earlier in the day, she had seen her mother sitting at the make-up table in her bedroom. She told her daughter that her mother had come to collect her. Sure enough, she died later that night.

George Best

One of the world's greatest ever footballers returned to comfort his loved ones from the other side, according to several British newspapers. *Daily Telegraph* columnist Celia Waldon said that the football star's widow Alex had told friends that the ghost of her husband had been with her in the family home on many occasions. George had been seen in his old chair by the fire and on several occasions had played tricks on his widow, although she is said to have found the experiences comforting.

The *Sun* and the *News of the World* ran similar stories involving other members of George Best's family and several of his friends, who are said to have had comforting communications from the footballer.

The British Royal Family

According to the book *The Prince and the Paranormal* by John Dale (W. H. Allen, 1986), back in 1953 the medium Lilian Bailey received a telephone call at her Wembley home. She was asked to give a sitting at a home in Kensington and was given a date and time to attend. When she arrived she was blindfolded and taken to the room, where she gave survival evidence through her spirit guide William Wotton, a captain of the Grenadier Guards who'd died during the First World War.

As soon as Lilian had finished her reading her blindfold was removed and she was shocked to see a royal audience before her. Attending the sitting were the Queen Mother (who had lost her husband King George VI just over a year earlier), the Queen, Prince Philip, the Duchess of Kent (whose husband had died in a plane crash in 1942) and the duchess's daughter, Princess Alexandra.

John Dale was given assistance with his book by both the queen's private secretary, Sir Martin Gilliat, and the Queen Mother. No objections were made to the story being included. (I believe the book is now out of print, but a quick search on the Internet revealed that second-hand books are still available at the time of writing.)

Queen Victoria also worked with a medium to communicate with her husband, the late Prince Albert. She secretly sent two courtiers to the home of Robert James Lees, whom a newspaper editor had reportedly witnessed being 'entranced' by the prince. The courtiers sat with Lees and immediately the prince came through, recognized them and gave them messages to pass back to the queen.

After that Lees gained the queen's confidence and was invited to give private sittings with her many times. She actually asked him if he would consider a permanent position as her personal medium. He politely declined, but not before advising the queen that he believed her personal servant at Balmoral, John Brown, was a natural medium and might be able to help her. Queen Victoria later developed a close relationship with Brown, probably as a result of his ability to connect her with her beloved Prince Consort. Much speculation surrounded their friendship, which eventually resulted in Victoria being given the nickname 'Mrs Brown'!

Cherie Burton

Australia's Housing Minister Cherie Burton told Australia's *Sunday Telegraph* that she was able to contact her dead grandfather through the American medium John Holland in 2003.

Cherie had a 20-minute private consultation with Holland, who she says gave her the nickname her grandfather had called her by – a name known only to Cherie and her grandfather, who had died six years earlier.

Neve Campbell

The Canadian *Scream* actress Neve Campbell has seen the spirit of her dead grandmother on several occasions, according to the magazine *People News*. Neve says that her father sees spirits all the time but the only loved one to make an appearance to her has been her grandmother.

Neve believes in the supernatural and says it's because of her Scottish roots. She says that lighting candles can provide a white light around you that will ward off evil – presumably in case the visiting spirit isn't a loving relative!

Hillary Clinton/Mahatma Gandhi/Eleanor Roosevelt

Hillary Clinton once attended mystical sessions with a 'new age guru', according to the book *The Choice* by Bob Woodward (Simon & Schuster, 1996). He claims that in 1995 a séance took place in the White House solarium and Hillary went into a trance and began 'channelling' the spirits of Mahatma Gandhi and Eleanor Roosevelt.

After Woodward published the story, Mrs Clinton and Jean Houston, her astrologer, who was present during the event, are both said to have downplayed the 'channelling', insisting that it was simply an 'imagined' conversation.

Toni Collette

The Australian actress, who is well known for her roles in *Muriel's Wedding* and *In Her Shoes* as well as a string of other films, used to sense her grandmother around her after she passed. She used to ask her not to talk to her, however, because she found the experience scary. She says that her father actually saw her grandmother's spirit on a couple of occasions.

Phil Collins

Phil Collins was born in London in 1951 – to play the drums! He became part of the group Genesis in 1970 and then pursued a solo career.

Phil believes that his late father watches over his family. He says that at one time his children's electric blankets were constantly being pulled from their beds overnight. He had the blankets checked out and it turns out they were faulty. A medium shed light on the mystery, telling Phil that his father was watching over his grandchildren.

Russell Crowe

The New Zealand-born actor had a strange experience in his kitchen one day when a kookaburra flew in and looked him straight in the eye. Russell knew immediately that this was a sign that his grandfather had passed away and right away telephoned his mother, who confirmed that he was correct.

Years later, Russell had a dream in which he was consoling his mother, who was in tears. As soon as he woke up he telephoned her. She answered the phone – in tears. She had been talking to an old friend of Russell's grandfather when the friend, without prompting, had mentioned that on the day of his passing she had received a visit from a kookaburra!

Engelbert Humperdinck/Jayne Mansfield

The house of the late actress Jayne Mansfield was bought by the singer Engelbert Humperdinck. Engelbert sensed the actress many times at the house, almost as if she were still keeping an eye on things. She used to make him aware of her rose-petal perfume. On one occasion he saw her in a long black dress, but wasn't frightened by her.

Michael Landon

According to the book *Amazing Psychic Experiences* by Julie Byron, actor Michael Landon once encountered the spirit of his deceased father. Landon was born in New York in 1936 and suffered the loss of his father, Eli Orowitz, when he was 24, shortly after he had received news that he'd won the role of 'Little Joe' in the show *Bonanza*.

Michael first felt his father's presence at his grave side. A hand touched his shoulder and he heard his father's voice reassuring him.

Later he went on to write the script for *Sam's Son*, a film about the love between a son and his father. He completed the script within three days and always believed that his father helped him with it, even going so far as to say that he heard him speaking to him whilst he was writing.

John Lennon/The Beatles/Liam Gallagher

John was tragically murdered at the entrance to the Dakota Building in New York in 1980. In life, the Beatles' singer had a very open mind when it came to the paranormal and once reported seeing a flying saucer. He and his wife Yoko also attended séances together.

Singer Liam Gallagher, of Oasis, insists that John has visited him from the other side. According to several sources, Liam was sleeping at a friend's house in Manchester one night when he felt the presence of John with him in the room.

After John's death, many of those who knew him talked about seeing or sensing his spirit. His son Julian is reported to have said that his father told him he would leave him a white feather to communicate with him once he'd passed over.

Whilst recording their song 'Free as a Bird' in 1995, the other Beatles band members, Sir Paul McCartney, George Harrison and Ringo Starr, sensed John in the studio and believed he appeared as a white peacock outside the building. Equipment kept playing up during the recording and there were suggestions of 'strange goings-on'.

Abraham Lincoln

The nineteenth-century US President had many paranormal experiences. He once described a dream to Mrs Lincoln and later to Ward Hill Lamon in which '*the* President in the White House' had been shot by an assassin. Amazingly, Lincoln himself was killed by an assassin shortly afterwards.

Although the President was thought not to believe in Spiritualism, Mrs Lincoln was interested in it and many mediums visited the White House during the couple's stay there. Mrs Lincoln's interest was fuelled by the tragic death of their 11-year-old son Willie, who died of bilious fever in 1862. President Lincoln apparently tolerated the séances, even watching on one occasion. According to the book *Myths after Lincoln* by Lloyd Lewis (Peter Smith Publishing, Inc., 1970), Mrs Lincoln found great comfort in the séances.

In a rather bizarre twist, the late President's own spirit is often sighted now, particularly at Ford's Theatre, where he was killed.

When Queen Wilhelmina of the Netherlands was once a guest of President Franklin D. Roosevelt, she heard a knock on her bedroom door. When she opened it she saw the ghostly figure of Abraham Lincoln looking down at her. She was so shocked that she literally fainted.

The British Prime Minister Winston Churchill visited the United States several times during World War II, on one occasion staying at the White House. There is a story that he stepped out of his bath one day 'wearing' only his 'cigar' and on walking to the adjoining bedroom saw President Lincoln leaning against the mantelpiece. According to one source, Churchill quipped, 'Good evening, Mr President. You seem to have me at a disadvantage.' Lincoln is said to have smiled, then disappeared.

Gillian McKeith

Nutritionist Gillian McKeith is well known for the TV shows where she turns around the lives of overweight people, including celebrities. Talking to the *Independent on Sunday,* Gillian revealed that after the death of her nephew and father, lights would flicker on and off in her home, objects would appear and disappear and she even heard unexplained voices. After all these experiences, she says she is now certain that there is life after physical death.

Kylie Minogue/Michael Hutchence

Australian singing sensation Kylie Minogue believes that she is protected by the spirit of her late boyfriend, singer Michael Hutchence, frontman of the 1980s pop band INXS. The story was reported on the website of TV medium Craig Hamilton-Parker. Kylie apparently feels Hutchence's presence very strongly when she is in need and says she finds it reassuring, though also a little scary.

Elvis Presley

Elvis, known to his fans as 'the King', has been seen by people all over the world since his passing in 1977. So many people have reported having paranormal experiences and sightings of the singer during near-death experiences, dreams and so on that a book has been written about it: *Elvis After Life* by Raymond Moody (Peachtree Publishers Ltd, 1987).

Elvis himself believed in an afterlife and it was something he often talked about. His step-brother David Stanley and mother Dee Presley are said to have made contact with him during a two-hour séance with the medium Dorothy Sherry. Elvis is reported to have spoken through housewife Dorothy, who hadn't been a particular fan of his during his lifetime, and during a trance sitting she is said to have produced many intimate details about him that were unknown to the public. She also related the exact words that the singer had spoken just days before he died. The relatives were apparently impressed with the communication, according to the website elvis-presley-forever.com.

I found the story of Dorothy Sherry's channelling of Elvis to be quite impressive and it is certainly worth further investigation if you are interested.

Robbie Williams/Ringo Starr

Singer Robbie Williams was born in Stoke-on-Trent in 1974. He became part of the famous boy band *Take That*, but by 1996 he was already pursuing his own career. Over time he has developed an interest in the paranormal. According to a source who reported to the *Daily Mirror*, Robbie took a keen interest in TV ghost shows at one point, even expressing the desire to have his own paranormal show.

For a while Robbie lived in the former home of Ringo Starr, the Beatles' drummer. He once gave an interview on Radio One about the spirits he'd seen there. He joked, 'When I moved out, the removal men wouldn't go in because of the old lady sitting in the chair.' Robbie also confessed that Ringo's son Zak Starkey had asked him if he'd seen the old lady and the 'children' in the garden. Robbie said he hadn't encountered the children.

This small selection of stories shows that afterlife contact can happen to everyone. Famous or not, most of us are interested in what happens next and have a great need to know that our loved ones are safe.

You know people occasionally write to tell me about deceased famous people coming to see them in dream visitations. Why might these well-known names do this? I honestly feel that it is a powerful way of reaching out to the living. I've said it before, but I was stunned by the number of people who've seen the late singer Elvis Presley or Princess Diana in visitation experiences and near-death experiences. However, if these people are able to bring you comfort by their presence at this time then you know they are going to try and help you if they can. What better work to be involved with on the other side than comforting the living?

On occasion well-known people will visit the living because as a spirit they have felt the grief that their passing has made on those who didn't know them in person. Television, radio, newspapers and the Internet bring people together in a way that was never experienced by earlier generations!

CHAPTER 11

Connecting to the Other Realms

What if you slept? And what if,
in your sleep, you dreamed?
And what if, in your dream, you went to heaven
and there plucked a strange and beautiful flower?
And what if, when you awoke,
you had the flower in your hand?
Ah, what then?

SAMUEL TAYLOR COLERIDGE

Despite the fact that so many millions of people around the world receive spontaneous communication from the other side of life, there are still those who believe it is wrong. Maybe there are religious reasons for their unwillingness to receive these blessings, or perhaps other members of the family are uncomfortable about paranormal phenomena. Yet our loved ones are visiting *us* and bringing messages of *love and comfort*. Can this be wrong?

Interestingly enough, I have recently started receiving afterlife contact stories where people tell me their loved ones have said, 'God arranged for me to visit you one last time,' or 'God told me I could come and say goodbye…'

Only you can decide if a visitation is something you wish to experience for yourself, but if you do, here are some suggestions that will encourage these loving visits to happen.

ENCOURAGING 'SPONTANEOUS' VISITATIONS FROM YOUR LOVED ONES

How do we get our loved ones to come to us? The simple answer is, you ask them to come and see you! OK, it's not always that simple, but many people have had success just by asking.

One lady told me, 'I asked God if he would let me see my husband one last time and he did.' Does this go against traditional religious beliefs? Many are now 'asking God,' 'asking the angels' or asking their loved ones directly if they will appear to them or bring them the much-needed signs that they are OK.

Many people have spontaneous visitation experiences whilst meditating and during dream sleep. You may well have already had a visitation. It's possible that reading this book will remind you of it. These experiences are positive and comforting.

Dream visitation is as safe as it gets. You don't need any equipment, there is nothing scary to do and it happens spontaneously over and over again. People all over the world talk to their loved ones in this way. It happens in every culture, to all ages, all religious backgrounds and both sexes. I've never heard of anyone being harmed when their loved ones popped over to say hi in a 'dream'.

Ways to make this happen

Will everyone receive a visitation or afterlife experience? No. There are many reasons why and why not. If you've ever heard the saying 'If you don't ask, you don't get,' then you'll understand better.

Want to try anyway? From the experiences of the thousands of people who have written to me, I have discovered some ways to do it:

- Talk to a photograph of your loved one. A photograph of the two of you is good, particularly one with a happy memory. If you don't have a photograph of the two of you together, then a photograph of your loved one on their own (or with others) will probably work just fine.

- If you don't have a photograph, hold an object which belonged to your loved one. (Jewellery is great, but other items can work too.) Feel their connection to the object whilst you make your request.

- If you have a recent item of clothing which belonged to the deceased, then work with this. The smell of a person is very powerful and this is a wonderful way of recalling the energy signature of your loved one.

- If you don't have a photo or anything that belonged to the deceased, don't worry. You don't have to *hold* anything. Just close your eyes and imagine your loved one standing in front of you. Talk to them as if they were with you (which I believe they are).

- Try to recall a happy time you spent together. Communication with your loved ones is very much about recalling that loving feeling you share. Love is the telephone line between the two sides of life.

- Write down your request if you want to. This might be in a special notebook or just on ordinary writing paper. Try placing your letter in an envelope and putting it under your pillow or keeping your notebook close to you when you sleep. I'm not suggesting that your loved one is going to read the actual letter (although I guess they might), but your intention is going to be more clearly received if you have literally 'spelled out' what you want and why. Those on the other side will *feel* and *hear* your message.

- Imagine yourself and your loved one being protected by a white loving energy. See this in your mind's eye as a fluffy white cloud surrounding you.

- Ask God (or the Goddess or your creator, whatever or whoever that is to you) to bring your loved one forward.

******

Whilst preparing this section of the book, I put the word out to my own loved ones in spirit and asked if they could visit *me*. I felt it would be helpful if I could receive some more information that I could pass on.

Well, I asked! During the course of writing the book I've had all sorts of things happen to me, especially whilst I've been sleeping. Most of my own visitation experiences (and I've had quite a few) have been when I have been on the verge of sleep, just before I've woken up or when I've had my usual night's sleep, woken up and then gone back to sleep again. This time, for a whole week I felt as if large sections of the book were given to me then. Although I remembered some of it when I woke up, in no time at all the facts had disappeared from my conscious memory. However, as soon as I sat down to write, the information was right there for me. That was great, but I wanted a personal dream visitation too. It had been so long since this had happened to me.

Then my sister Debbie called me and said, 'We have to get together, your father-in-law has been to visit me again!' I couldn't wait to have a chat and she was so excited. My father-in-law Jack died nearly 20 years ago and my sister had met him a few times at family events when John and I were first married.

She told me, 'I was having a really boring, normal dream when all of a sudden I could see him in the background walking close to me and then moving away...' I told her that he was waiting for permission to enter her dream and chat! She asked him over and the dream had been very lucid, realizing that he had come to visit her as a spirit, rather than as part of a 'normal' dream.

The first thing my sister remembered was that as it had been a hot evening and she had pushed the covers off the bed, she was naked. She told him, 'I have nothing on!'

He immediately dismissed this and reassured her, saying, 'I can see nothing.' Then he changed the subject. He was always so polite in life too!

She asked him, 'Why have you come to see me and not Jacky or John?'

He explained, 'When John goes to bed he goes to sleep, nothing more. He closes everything else off.'

My husband admits that he never even remembers ordinary dreams.

Jack continued, 'Jacky sleeps on another level and I can't reach her.'

Well, I have no idea what this 'other level' is, but it's not the first time I've heard this explanation from a spirit.

It explains a lot, doesn't it? People often say with their own family experiences, 'Why did that person get a visit instead of me?' Now we have another explanation for why this doesn't or does happen: our sleep pattern has to be appropriate for our loved ones to communicate with us. The bad news is that I'm not sure how we can change that. However, you can still encourage contact in the ways I mentioned earlier.

My father-in-law and sister went on to have quite a long conversation and she asked him a lot of questions about her own life. Some things he was able to help her with and other personal life-path questions were answered with 'I'm not at liberty to say.' Spirits can't always tell us what's happening next. Sometimes we have yet to choose the path or it's not set in stone. So you could say that there is no 'correct' answer as to what we should do with our lives – it's up to us what *we* decide.

Before he left, my father-in-law sent his love to his granddaughters (who were born after he died) and Debbie said sadly to him, 'You'll miss the eighteenth birthday party.' He replied, 'No, I'll be there.'

Debbie said at that point she woke up without having the chance to say goodbye. She felt the experience was very positive and it was as if my father-in-law was helping her out as well as using her as a (willing) messenger for me.

I know that he was trying to give me an important message for the book: that some of us, especially children, are naturally able to receive dream visitation experiences, while others, like me, are not so easy to reach.

The good news is that even though I apparently 'sleep on a different level', I have experienced many dream visitations from people I knew in life. So many people have. I went for a coffee with a friend today and she told me about a 'strange dream' in which her great grandma visited her. She said, 'She looked so young and fit and we met at a grand house. I knew she was dead, because I mentioned it. She came to give me a message about a family ring.'

WHAT TO EXPECT

Some of the things you might expect if you ask for a visit:

- You might get a dream visitation in which your deceased loved one appears.

- You might get a dream visitation in which another loved one appears (if the person you want to contact is not able to visit at that time).

- Your loved one might pass a message for you through another relative (as with my sister and me), who will tell you, 'I had a strange dream the other night…'

- You might have a 'dream' experience in which a memory is replayed or a message is given.

- You might experience something in that trance state between sleeping and waking, perhaps a person is sitting on the bed with you or standing in the room.

- A simple sign might appear in your waking life: you find a white feather; a picture of your loved one moves or falls over; you find a letter or a piece of jewellery or similar which connects you and your deceased loved one; you come across an associated smell or piece of music, and so on.

- You might feel or sense your loved one around you over the next few days or weeks. When this happens, it can seem as if time stands still. You might feel very cold, particularly warm or perhaps as though your clothes are full of static electricity.

- You might hear your name or another short phrase whispered. Again, sometimes this will happen in that sleep/awake trance stage of sleep.

******

Classic dream visitation signs

How do you know this is real? Have you already had a visitation? Do you recognize any of these signs?

- In the 'dream' our loved one appears younger than when they died, at their peak of fitness or health, or how they wish they had looked (thinner, for example). They come looking at their best – but we still recognize them, of course.

- Illness and bodily disabilities are no longer apparent, or we are shown 'before' and 'after' images so that we can see that they are fit and well. If Granddad lost a leg in the war, he will have two legs now. If your aunty lost her hair during cancer treatment, she will probably show herself with long shiny hair. Even the mental disabilities of the body no longer exist.

- We know they are dead and might even ask them about it with the classic comment: 'But you're dead, aren't you?'

- They wear clothes we recognize – possibly what they were buried in or something we bought them – or things that are familiar or comforting to us – the jumper that brought out the colour of their eyes, their best suit, etc.

- They may communicate – usually with thoughts rather than by moving their mouth – or not, but they always bring a sense of love and peace.

- They appear full of vitality or fizzing with energy, sometimes surrounded by a white or golden light.

- Sometimes they will have a guardian angel or spiritual guide in the background. (I believe the guardians are always there but don't always show themselves.)

- Sometimes we can touch them, and when we do they feel real. At other times this is not possible, as touching them brings a breaking down of the vibrational energy that is used to create the visual image.

- They either appear behind some sort of barrier – a gate, hedge, door, etc. – or leave that way. We are usually not allowed to pass through this barrier.

******

Depending on the skill of the soul communicating, the places where we 'visit' them can vary greatly. In its simplest form, a dream visitation would consist of a bare room with two chairs. You might be sitting on a chair and your loved one might just walk into the room and sit down. Sometimes they will take you to a 'mock-up' of a place that the two of you visited together in the past or a home that one or other of you lived in. People have met loved ones in a tepee, sitting round a campfire, in their old house, in a bar, in a wood, in a grocery shop (that was one of mine!), on a staircase or in a multi-storey car park (symbols of the different levels which separate our dimensions) and many more places besides.

If they have the ability to create a welcoming place for you, your loved ones can use quite ingenious ways to get you there. Sometimes a normal dream will shift into a visitation when your loved one knocks on your dream door, rings your dream doorbell or even calls you on a dream telephone!

How can we get this to happen more often?

- Knowing that it is possible to bring about a connection can actually help to bring one about. Fear can be an inhibitor, however.

- If you want to see Grandma one last time but on the other hand you are terrified that she might actually appear, she probably won't! Grandma knows best in this instance and will probably just bring you a more subtle sign. When you are ready for this to happen, it probably will.

- Make yourself comfortable before asking your relatives to come. Perhaps ask for a visit when there are others in the house with you, or out with you. Sharing your experience will help a lot.

- If you do feel you've had a visit or a sign, say, 'Thank you for my sign.' That way your loved one will say, 'Ah, OK, that worked, so I'll try that again…'

******

RELAXATION TECHNIQUES

Remember we talked about how our loved ones find it easier to reach us when we are daydreaming, on the verge of sleep or even in a coma? During these altered states of consciousness our minds are more open to receiving loving feelings and mind-to-mind contact from the other realms. Let's try another safe method of meeting people from the other side.

If you have ever tried meditation you might find that these relaxation techniques work well for you. Even if you haven't, give them a go! Practice makes perfect.

What we are doing here is finding another way of opening up the mind. There are psychics and mediums who do a great job of contacting the other side, but I don't want you to have to rely on someone else. If you can move on with your life because you can get a sense that your loved one has safely made it to heaven, then I believe that you're going to be happier.

Your safe 'imaginary' meeting-place

With this method, the trick is to create an 'imaginary' place of your own choosing. You create this special place in your mind. Rather than wait for the bare room with two chairs scenario, or wherever your loved one decides, *you* create the space and they come to you.

Although the place is 'imaginary' in our world, it will become *real* in other realities. You can visit it over and over again in your mind, and the more you work on creating it, the stronger the image will become.

Your imagination is a strong creative force – what you create in your mind you can manifest in life (slowly) and in heaven (much more quickly). The heavenly realms are based on different realities from our own. Many of the places there are built using 'thought creation'. Even in our own reality we create an image in our mind first of all before we manifest it into 'solid' reality. What we call 'imagination' is not 'made up', it's 'thought creation'. There is a difference! It *is* real, but in a different time and space.

Your special heavenly space might be a beach, a wood, a garden, a room or even a bar! Let's have a look at an example so you can see what I mean. Let's have a go at a woodland. If you are great at visualization (seeing pictures in your mind), you can probably get this quite quickly.

If you can't 'see' your space in your mind, don't worry, just *know* that it's real and bring in other senses if you can – sights, sounds, smells, touch and feelings. A real world is created by many senses; sight is just one of them.

> Start with the size of your woodland. What does it look like? How many trees are there? What sort are they? Are there other plants? What sort of flowers are there? Are there animals? Birds? Can you hear the birds singing? Is there a stream or a lake? Can you hear the water? Smell the flowers? How old are the trees? Can you hold your hands in the water, touch the trees? Would a butterfly land on your hand or a bird sit next to you? Is there a seat where you can sit down, or perhaps a fallen log? Is there grass in your wood? A picnic table? Is the sun shining?

You can just visualize these things in your mind or write a list or, if you want more help, cut pictures from magazines and create a physical collage first. Do anything you want to help form the images in your mind.

Take your time with this. You may want to build your 'mind space' over several weeks. Each time you go back there you can add more details. You know, the really surprising thing is that each time you close your eyes and start to work on your meeting place again, you will remember where you left it! The more you do this, the more detailed your space becomes. Have fun. Add your favourite flowers, scents and so on. Make it a place that you're going to love visiting over and over again.

Now what?

Preparing your 'outer' space

Once you have a safe place in your mind, you'll want to feel safe in your physical surroundings too. What do you need? You might like to:

- Sit in a comfortable chair

- Sit with your back to a wall

- Arrange comfortable lighting in your room

- Close the curtains

- Play gentle and relaxing music

- Make sure you are alone in the house

- Or arrange for people to be in the house when you perform your meditation

- Perform this relaxation exercise alongside others (in the same room)

- Take the phone off the hook

- Lock the door

- Wear comfortable clothing (your temperature might drop a little if you fall asleep whilst you do this, so you may want to cover your arms and wear socks to keep warm)

- Ask a friend to read the visualization to you

- Record the visualization and play it back

- Remember the visualization and just do it roughly as I have suggested, creating your own variations as you go along.

******

There may be other things that you need. If so, do get them. Feeling happy in your surroundings is important. If you like, you can burn a favourite aromatherapy candle in the room. Make sure it is in a safe holder or, even better, use a scented tea light or safety candle or choose a candle in a glass holder, otherwise you will be worrying about your candle the whole time and not relaxing at all. You might also wish to use an aromatherapy burner (follow the instructions on your package) and add one or two drops of essential oil, usually mixed with water, in the well at the top.

Scents have a vibration and, as we have seen, our loved ones often bring a scent as a sign that they are around us. Therefore it makes sense that the vibration of certain fragrances will work to help the communication. If you are using scents in your room, always use natural aromatherapy oils (which come from plant and flower essences). The scent has to be one you like, of course. You won't be very relaxed if you hate the smell in the room! If you're not sure, try:

- Lavender

- Rose

- Frankincense.

******

I have found frankincense to be particularly powerful, but not everyone likes the smell. Remember that whatever makes *you* feel good is the perfect scent to use.

This part of your visualization will help you to relax. Relaxation is hard if you are tired, anxious, etc., but do not do this exercise if you have taken mood-altering drugs or alcohol. You need to be physically well and in good mental health. Aim to work on this for around 20 minutes or so, building up to longer sessions with practice.

Take your time with your visualization, especially with filling your body with light, and imagine the 'feel-good' feelings flooding through your body. Read slowly.

Ready?

Meet your loved one in a relaxation visualization

Start by imagining yourself surrounded by a loving white light. See this as the light of all love and protection. It is going to act as your guide and lead you to your special place. See it inside and outside your body. Imagine it right now… Feel the light … feel the light…

Direct this energy until it flows into every part of your body. See the light fill your shoulders … arms … hands … fingers… See the light fill your head and neck … flooding down through your chest… down your spine … into your stomach… See the light flooding down through your thighs …your calves, your ankles and your feet and toes…

Imagine yourself filled with perfect bliss. Feel this energy flooding through your body. Bliss, bliss … bliss. Feel the energy of bliss…

Imagine yourself filled with perfect love. Feel this energy flooding though your body. Love, love … love. Feel the energy of love…

Imagine yourself filled with perfect peace. Feel this energy flooding through your body. Peace, peace ... peace. Feel the energy of peace...

Imagine now the energy of perfect calm. Feel this energy flooding through your body. Calm, calm ... calm... Feel it now...

Keep imagining these feelings until you feel relaxed. Your music and other things will help you here.

When you are ready, see a beautiful gilded gate in front of you. Open it and move through it... Start to float towards your special place – your beach or wood or whatever this is for you.

Sit or stand in your space as you wish. Start to look around you. Recall all the details. Make it as real as you can.

When you are ready, invite your loved one to visit you. (Remember that we can invite whomever we like, but it might not be possible for a specific person to attend at this time. Be ready for another deceased loved one to bring a message for you or your own guardian angel or spiritual guide to step forward.)

Stay as long as you wish. Listen to what is being said, ask questions if you want or just soak up the loving feelings.

When you are ready, float back through the gate, closing it behind you, and into your physical room.

In your own time, open your eyes.

Have a warm drink and a light snack – perhaps a biscuit – to ground yourself back in the here and now.

What is likely to happen?

At first you might not experience anything at all. That's fine, but do try this a few times before you dismiss it altogether. The chances are that you are not relaxed enough. Many people will have experiences whilst simply doing the ironing or washing up(!), so it's not hard to achieve. You just need to be relaxed.

You might sense your loved one's energy around you, feel their presence, see them or even hear them. Just enjoy what comes. They might sit back for a while, waiting till the right time. This will be new for them too!

Here are some common questions:

Q. *What happens if I get scared?*
A. Just open your eyes and stop the experience. Try again another time.

******

Q. *What happens if I get lost during the experience? Will I get stuck?*
A. No, of course not. This is a visualization and you

use visualization all day long, for example when you imagine what your steak might taste like with pepper sauce on it or how your new curtains will go with your sofa!

******

Q. *Can I go too deeply into the visualization?*

A. No. If you are relaxed you might stay for longer than you intended because you are enjoying the relaxation time, that's all. If you get very relaxed, you might fall asleep. There is no problem with either of these. Eventually, when you are rested, you will wake up again!

******

Q. *What if I see something negative?*

A. It is important that you are happy and relaxed when you start. So if you are anxious before you begin your visualization, you might create something in your mind to stop you completing this happy experience, in the same way that when we are worried about any new experience in normal waking life we might have a bad dream or nightmare. If you are worried at any time, open your eyes and just stop. You are in complete control at all times. Try another day and build up your experience in

your own time. There's no need to rush this.
You are in charge.

******

Q. *What if I see nothing at all?*
A. Enjoy the relaxing experience and try again another
time.

******

Q. *Does this work for everyone?*
A. For most people eventually, yes.

******

Q. *Are there any after-effects?*
A. The relaxation techniques should leave you feeling
positive and happy. If you have a 'meeting' visitation
experience, then you might shed a few tears of
happiness. You might feel a little frightened, as you
would with anything new, but that will soon pass
when you realize you are connecting to someone
you know and love. Their energy will be just as you
remember it. They won't hurt you! Just do as much
or as little as you want to and then stop.

Some people find that once they have tried this experience other spiritual signs happen in the days and weeks that follow. Have a read through the visitation stories in this book to see the sort of signs your loved ones might bring you. If you are unhappy with them at any time, just ask for them to stop.

I think I will give Sam the last word here. She dropped me an e-mail to share some of her own experiences:

'I read a book, then had the experiences'

I started reading one of your books, An Angel by my Side, *a few weeks ago. I had read the first few pages, in which you describe how spirits often communicate, but had not yet got to the part where you talk about how they sometimes interfere with electrical devices. For some reason I decided to go into the kitchen. I noticed a strong burning smell and discovered that it was the dishwasher. A knife had broken through the bottom of the cutlery holder and the handle had melted at the bottom. After sorting it out I carried on reading your book and got to the part about electrical interference, so knew it was a sign! That was the first of three things that happened to me over the next few days.*

The second experience was the smell. I was in a rush and on my way out of the house I had to nip upstairs.

To my surprise, all I could smell was pot pourri in every room! I don't have pot pourri in the house, or any kind of air freshener upstairs, but the smell was very powerful. I thought it was a bit odd at the time, but it was only the next day, when I read about smells accompanying spirit visitations, that it all became clear.

Then I had the third experience. My mum died 20 years ago this March, when I was 13 years old. I have often 'felt' her with me over the years, especially over the last five years, but one night I felt her hug me in a dream. I know I was dreaming, because I was in bed asleep, but the hug was very real and I felt it. I told her I loved her and I felt very happy to have her with me again after nearly 20 years.

It was the next day that I read in your book about visitations and how these can sometimes happen when we are in a 'dream state'.

I have not yet finished your book, but am looking forward to any other signs I may be shown.

So, if you want a visitation experience, remember that just reading a book about them will make them more likely to happen! (OK, so I couldn't resist having the last word after all!)

CHAPTER 12

In Celebration of Life

That which is bitter to endure
may be sweet to remember.

THOMAS FULLER

One of the hardest things to bear after losing a loved one is the feeling that you have not had the opportunity to say goodbye. Naturally it's impossible to be with every family member when they cross over – I mean, it's just never going to happen – but when a loss is sudden we often feel that we have missed closure. We feel cheated out of a special moment with our loved one.

There are lots of things that we can do to ease this pain. Have a look though the methods listed in this chapter and see if there is anything that you feel might help you.

Naturally loss brings about deep feelings of grief, and grief is what consumes us in the first weeks and months after death. Many people find the first week or so passes in a daze, but having lots of things to do – making funeral arrangements, organizing bank accounts, sorting through belongings, and so on – can help in a way. Later, when personal details are sorted, many find they need a project, something to help them with the next stage of grief. Celebrating the life of the loved one and finding a way of commemorating their existence can help ease the pain.

Here are some ideas to help you celebrate the life of your loved one. These suggestions might be things that you wish to carry out alone or share with others who have been honoured to have known this special person.

A BOOK OF LIFE MEMORIES

Your loved one meant a lot to you and always will. Have you considered making a 'memories book' about them? Several members of the family could help you with this, either by working on their own book or working on one with you.

Things you might like to add to your book:

- Photographs with special memories

- Poems and special thoughts – both those written by others and those you have created yourself

- Letters or printed e-mails you have shared

- Tickets, invitations and so on relating to special events you enjoyed together

- Lists of music or song lyrics which meant a lot to you both

- Memories of special occasions you shared – happy times, sad times, moving times. Write them down.

- Pressed flowers or leaves from funeral bouquets

- Pictures of places with special memories for the two of you (try travel brochures, the Internet, magazine articles and so on for suitable images)

- Listings for favourite TV programmes or films

- If the person is a friend, work colleague or sports team member you might want to include group photographs and details of team achievements as well as special memories of individuals.

- Ask people what your loved one meant to them. You might be surprised to discover ways in which they touched the lives of others.

- Decorate your book with stickers; decoupage photographs (Victorian women used to cut out pictures of flowers/

figurines, etc., and glue them together on household objects to create a new image); use paints and coloured pencils and felt pens to illustrate your pages or around the edges of poems and thoughts.

- Write down any signs and any paranormal visitations too, both your own and those received by others. Let people know you are recording them. By keeping a record of these types of experiences you actually encourage more!

******

I would suggest that you collect all of these things separately and then either add them to a scrapbook (bought or made) or assemble your pages afterwards. You can use a loose-leaf binder or buy heavyweight paper from an art shop, hole-punch the pages and bind them with ribbon. This allows you to dictate the numbers of pages and also makes it easy to add to your book as you go along. Don't forget to make a beautiful cover too.

Find a way of keeping your precious book safe. Maybe make a slipcover or find or make a box to keep it in. Your book could take pride of place at an event to mark your loved one's life at a later date.

A CELEBRATION OF LIFE PARTY

The Mexicans enjoy a day they call 'the Day of the Dead' (Día de los Muertos) on which they commemorate all lost family members. The day, 2 November, is a national holiday and a time of festivities rather than of mourning. Families will create an altar in their homes containing flowers, food, photographs and objects associated with or belonging to deceased loved ones. The idea is that the spirit of their loved ones will be attracted to these objects and return to join in the celebrations and feastings.

If loved ones are buried nearby, a path of flowers (or petals) is laid from the grave side to the house to guide the dead back home. Traditionally children are remembered on the first day, the Day of the Little Angels (Día de los Angelitos) and adults are commemorated on the second day. Special foods like bread, cakes and sweets are made using symbols of death (skeletons and gravestones, for example). Food is either shaped into these symbols, or toys in the shape of skeletons, etc., are included as part of the decoration.

This might not appeal to you, but I'm sure you can work out your own variation on a celebration of life gathering. However you choose to do it, find your own way of commemorating your loved one's life. It makes more sense of death.

Twelve months after a passing, many people would be ready to organize a 'celebration of life' party to remember their loved one. This event could be small or big, depending on your needs. Of course it might not be appropriate to hold an event on the date of the person's passing, but another date might work well, a birthday, for example; or why not consider following the Mexicans and hold your event on 2 November?

This would not be a morbid event but a loving one. Relatives might want to light a candle or read special words or poems to commemorate the life of the person. You could take it in turn to tell a fun story relating to your relationship with them. This would be the perfect opportunity to bring out your book of memories or a collage of happy photographs that could be displayed around the room.

Don't forget to include refreshments. Maybe guests would enjoy bringing contributions of food or drink in a kind of 'pot luck' supper? The last thing you want is for the event to become overwhelming and too much work for you. A family picnic, tea party, pizza get-together or fish and chip supper could work better for you. Make up your own 'rules'.

Although tears are inevitable, remember this is a happy occasion to celebrate life, not death. Perhaps a glass of something alcoholic would be in order – if this is part of your normal family celebrations!

A REMEMBRANCE GARDEN AND OTHER OUTDOOR SPACES

All over the world, institutes and communities have created gardens of remembrance to contemplate and focus on lost loved ones. The Chinese have a spring festival, part of which involves a process called 'saluting the tomb'. They cover graves in peeled eggs and red rice and burn money for the dead. The Japanese have a festival that involves feasting. Graves are cleaned and boats are floated onto water to carry away the souls of the dead. And Nepal has a special day when fathers both living and dead are remembered. The deceased are commemorated all over the world.

You could organize a special day when you visit the grave or a nominated space, maybe planting spring flowers or bulbs if you are allowed to, or perhaps creating a whole garden in celebration. Friends may enjoy contributing by bringing along seeds or plants from their own gardens.

I remember when a young fireman died in my local community, the firefighters created a special garden in the grounds of the fire station.

You might enjoy creating a living, breathing space of your own. Here are some ideas:

- Plant a tree (perhaps adding a commemorative plaque)

- Plant a rose

- Plant up a pot (a lovely idea for children) and decorate it with angel or fairy plant sticks

- If you have the room, section off a part of your garden where you can sit and remember your loved one. Add a bench or seat of some sort and include lights, a statue or maybe a bird table or birdbath. Other ways of bringing interest to your space include planting flowers that attract butterflies or bees.

******

It's not always easy to visit a grave on a regular basis. But spirits tell me, 'We're not there anyway!' The spirits of our loved ones are attracted to *our energy*, not the place where their bodies lie. Create your own beautiful place.

Your natural place might even be your mantelpiece, if you regularly place flowers in a pretty jug and stand it next to a photograph of your loved one. That way you can *both* enjoy the flowers every day.

OTHER IDEAS

How else might you celebrate the life of your loved one?

- Write a book about them.

- Approach a magazine or newspaper about the possibility of being interviewed about them. Are there lessons to be learned from their death, or life? Do you have special memories that might be of interest to others?

- Raise funds in the name of your loved one – life-saving baby equipment for your local hospital; audio books for hearing-impaired, etc.

- Start your own charity.

- Run a race for charity or join in a charity event.

******

Using your energy in a positive way like this is very healing. And you know that your loved one will be proud of what you are doing in their name.

REMEMBERING ANIMALS

For many people, the loss of a pet can be as difficult as the loss of a human friend. You may wish to commemorate your pet by following some of these suggestions.

When my little dog passed away, I kept her bed, a wicker shopping basket, and planted it up with a selection of bedding plants, ivy and lavender. It sits in my garden and is a wonderful way of remembering her life. If you're short on space, maybe a small window box with animal figurines as decoration might be something you would consider.

If you are good on the computer, how about creating a website in your pet's honour? You can include photographs and special memories. Perhaps you could add pages where others could add memories of their own pets. You could also add poems and links to other useful websites.

Do you have a lot of photographs of your pet? How about creating a collage of images in a pretty frame? Is there a local artist who would paint a portrait of your pet from a favourite photograph? You could keep a little notebook with special memories or sketches, sponsor a bench with a plaque... The list is endless.

Remember, people all over the world receive messages and visits from their pets after they have died. If you've heard your dog bark or your horse has appeared to you in a dream, write it down and celebrate your special memories of life and the afterlife.

Celebrating a life is a healing and healthy thing to do and you will find your own way of doing it. It needn't be anything big. Small gestures are perfect too.

CHAPTER 13

'Afterlife' Letters

*One cannot help but be in awe when he
contemplates the mysteries of eternity, of life,
of the marvellous structure of reality. It is enough
if one tries to merely comprehend a little of this
mystery every day.*

ALBERT EINSTEIN

Every month I receive hundreds of letters and e-mails about afterlife contact. Over the years I've learned a lot about the phenomenon and do try and reply to everyone when I can, although, as you can imagine, this gets harder as the number of letters increases!

Here is a little glimpse of a few recent letters. I have kept all the writers anonymous, but the questions are all real ones received through my website. My answers are based on my many years of studying afterlife communication

251

and the thousands of stories I've received, as well as my own personal experiences. I hope you might find the answers to some of your own questions here. Bear in mind, though, that there is never an ultimate right or wrong answer, so when reading my replies please take the answers that feel right to you and ignore those that don't fit with your personal or religious beliefs.

Q. *My son Scott died suddenly 10 years ago. I would love to hear from him or have some contact with him. I know an afterlife does exist, as I've had contact from another friend who died.*

My wife and I are members of a Spiritualist church and I am convinced she is gifted. She hears things, sees lights and has sensations that she attributes to Scott. I am beginning to believe Scott does not want to contact me and it is very distressing.

I went to see a well-recommended Spiritualist privately, but she said there was no one waiting to contact me and lapsed into generalities. I love to hear the contacts people have in church and my wife's sensations thrill me, but I am so sad about not receiving anything. I visit my son's grave daily and talk to him all the time, so he must know that I have not forgotten him. Can it be that I am just not attuned to the spirit world? Can you advise me on what I could do?

A. I am so sorry about your sad loss. It seems wrong for an adult to outlive their own child and this type of loss is particularly hard to live with.

It is difficult to know why one person receives a visitation and others do not, but our spirit friends have given me some clues. One soul told his friend on this side of life that he had 'tried to visit other people but as they were so sad they could not see him'. It's as if our grief closes down our psychic senses in some way. When this happens it is often children or friends outside our immediate circle who are able to pick up a message, although there is no guarantee that they will pass this message on to you, of course.

Many people do find mediums helpful, but as you are working through a 'third party' your relatives may not want to or be able to communicate with them. Not all mediums are genuine (although I am not saying this is the case here, naturally), but do be wary. You did the right thing by visiting someone who was recommended.

As you are still visiting the grave daily, I can feel your pain is still very strong. We all grieve in our own way (there is no 'wrong' or 'right' way to do this), but do remember that your son is connected to you personally and not especially to the site of his burial. You could talk to a photograph of him in your own home and the connection would be just as strong as if you were to go to the grave, if not stronger.

In the meantime, continue to enjoy the messages that are passed through your wife. I feel sure they are meant to be a comfort to you both.

******

Q. *When my mother-in-law passed away it was a very cold April, but there was a butterfly, a Red Admiral, in the bedroom where she died. I can remember looking at it and not remembering seeing it there before, even though I had been sitting with her for hours before she finally passed away.*

The day of her funeral was very cold, but in the crematorium, on the wall beside the vicar, there was the same type of butterfly – a 'coincidence', I thought.

Years later I was in the labour ward delivering my son. It was a cold November day and just as he came into the world everyone in the room looked at the clock on the wall to make sure of his birth time. There on the clock was another Red Admiral butterfly! At the time I distinctly remember smelling my mother-in-law's perfume too.

A year later, on my son's first birthday, it came as no surprise to us that there was a butterfly in the living room beside his birthday cards!

The butterflies have continued to this day.
The day my father-in-law passed away the same
type of butterfly was in the living room where he
died, and the same thing happened at a recent
wedding.

Now whenever I see a Red Admiral butterfly I
think of my mother-in-law and wonder if she's
just popped in for a visit. We were very close and
it's nice to think that even if we can't have our
usual chats she can still keep an eye on things.
The other side communicates in all sorts of ways
and this is hers.

A. I thoroughly enjoyed reading about your butterfly experiences. In some parts of the world, butterflies are seen as spirits. Other common signs are moths and dragonflies, so your mother-in-law's choice was perfect.

I have received many amazing stories of butterflies following along in funeral cars and landing on people's hands at the graveside. There was one beautiful story of a dragonfly that landed on a lady's lips whilst she was tending the grave of her young son. Dragonflies were the symbol that the family associated with him. Like your butterflies, they visited them over and over again.

Of course a cynic would say that these were coincidences, but often a butterfly can appear on a window right in front of your face as you are talking about the deceased or even fly out of a locked cupboard. Timing is everything and your own stories are perfect examples of how our loved ones send their messages at the perfect time, just so we know for sure.

******

Q. *About five years ago a very close family friend, whom I classed as an uncle, passed away. Since he died I have carried the guilt of not attending his funeral. I was pregnant with my second child at the time and my granddad felt it would be too upsetting for me to attend. I'd really like to know that my uncle has forgiven me and whether he has seen the two sons I have had after his death.*

A. Please do not give this another thought. There is nothing to forgive. We often feel guilty after a loved one dies; it is normal when we can't be present at the funeral or the death itself. But it is impossible to be with every family member or friend during these times – sometimes even if we truly want to be there or try very hard to, it still isn't going to happen! What is important is that we give as much as we can during life and then forgive ourselves, going forward with no regrets.

Our loved ones won't be holding any grudges, whatever happened during life or after death.

When they pass over they are aware of the love and loss of those who are left behind. They feel this information in the same way that we still feel the love between us. Love doesn't die when someone passes over. So your friend will know that you cared for him deeply and still do.

Many souls still take an interest in our lives after they cross, but not in the way you might think. Some people worry that their deceased loved ones are watching their private moments, but they aren't. The connection is at a soul level. So they usually know about our achievements, new members of the family, and so on. In fact young children often see their grandparents, aunts and uncles, even when they never met in life! Strange, isn't it?

******

Q. *I'm only 16 and my mum told me that you probably wouldn't give advice to someone so young, but I thought I would try anyway.*

My brother died last year and almost every member of my family has been contacted by him or given signs to prove he is there, but I haven't. We were really close and I was very protective of him and it hurts me so much that he doesn't think I'm ready to see him.

*My mum went to a psychic a few months
ago and I begged to go, but I wasn't allowed.
My brother communicated with her that night.
She said that he told her to tell me he is always
with me, but that isn't enough. My mum and dad
feel him all around our house, but I don't feel him
anywhere.*

A. Thank you for writing to me. I can't imagine how
sad you must be feeling right now and of course
frustrated too. I know that at 16 you probably feel
much older than people realize. I am sure you also
feel very left out – I know I would.

You don't need to see a psychic, though – I
doubt very much it would help you, to be honest –
as you can ask your brother to visit you himself.
In fact, he probably already is doing so.

Do know, though, that you might not always be
able to sense or feel him around you. This is not
your fault. Don't give up, though. I'm sure you will
sense something when the time is right.

******

Q. *I have been reading about your work, which has
been a great comfort to me since I lost my cousin
just over a month ago. Sally had been depressed
for some time and was on various drugs and
therapies to treat her 'chemical imbalance'.*

She was in immense emotional pain and I think she felt she simply couldn't hang on any longer, so she killed herself, which was an awful shock.

I would like to think that she is OK now and no longer in pain. However, I am also a bit concerned that she might be punished in some way for taking her own life. (This probably stems from religious indoctrination.) Some religions have a belief that the soul of a person who takes their own life does not pass on to the other side and is in an eternal state of limbo and discomfort.

Do you have any information regarding this subject that might clarify things for me? Is the soul of a person who takes their own life treated any differently from the soul of a person who dies naturally or accidentally?

A. I am so sorry. Losing a loved one under any circumstances is hard, but suicide brings its own difficulties for those left behind. What I can do is give you my opinion based on the many years of research that I have done, and you have to take from this what feels right to you and, as with all of my answers, leave anything which does not feel right in terms of your own belief system.

Yes, I believe that the soul who takes their own life is treated a little differently. Your cousin will no longer be in physical pain – I want to reassure you of that. She will, however, clearly need extra healing and assistance, and will get plenty. She will also be given plenty of support, love and understanding.

It is common for the soul to experience regret almost immediately after attempting suicide (in fact those that get pulled back from the brink of death nearly always report this feeling).

Of course, when a soul is in a body which has chemical imbalances, it is so hard. It's often a more difficult life choice than they realized when they started out. But there is no punishment as such for ending that life. After death the soul will review their life just as others do and will see how they might do things differently another time. We all make mistakes – it is human.

Your cousin will be given the aid that she needs so that reincarnation (the return of the soul to a new life) can take place as soon as she has recovered. With this sort of passing I believe that reincarnation often occurs more quickly than after a natural death, but it does vary a lot. All in all, I want to reassure you that your cousin will be given plenty of care and understanding in the heavenly realms.

******

Q. *Does a specific time have to elapse before my mum can come to visit me from heaven?*

A. Sometimes the souls of our loved ones can appear

to us in the short time *before* physical death (whilst they are in a coma, for example) or even immediately after death. It varies such a lot, though, and other souls may not visit us for over a year or not ever. This can sometimes be due to the healing that is occurring or the special roles that they have to play on other side. They may be busy in other locations helping other souls, for example.

When someone can't visit us, it is possible to receive contact from other relatives who have passed over and wish to reassure us that our loved one is fine and has arrived safely. This is most likely to happen in a dream visitation experience.

******

Q. *We have just lost a dear aunt and my sister-in-law had to go to her house to clear away her personal things. Just as she pulled up onto the drive she clearly heard a ringing of bells. There is no church nearby. What does this signify?*

A. Victorians often used to report the ringing of bells in séance rooms when mediums were trying to connect to the other side, although I don't hear of this phenomenon much nowadays.

Our loved ones will bring a whole variety of experiences for us to enjoy, including the scent of flowers and tobacco, knocking sounds, the ringing of doorbells and flashing of house lights. Each phenomenon in isolation may mean little, but when several are experienced over time, it may be an afterlife contact.

If your sister feels that the bells were a sign from your aunt, then it's possible that they were. Sometimes it's just down to personal interpretation. No one else has the benefit of the feelings which were experienced at the actual time of the phenomenon.

******

Q. *I need some sort of confirmation that I am not daft. Although I am 32, I am one of the few people to reach my age without losing someone close to them and suffering grief.*

When the TV presenter Steve Irwin died I was shocked and upset and also quite perturbed by how I was feeling about someone I had not known personally. These feelings continued for approximately six weeks. I couldn't stop thinking about the sadness of it all and how devastated his family must be and what a waste and why take someone like him who was doing all he could to change the world and how we thought about our precious animals. These thoughts were all-consuming.

One night I was fast asleep and in my dream I was walking my dogs. I felt warm and comforted as a strange person was approaching me and then I realized it was Steve Irwin. He just stayed for a few seconds and said, 'I am OK.' I got the feeling that he was in a hurry because there were a lot of people he had to see and all he wanted to do was get back to his family.

The reality of the dream was unlike anything I had ever experienced before and I felt so much better when I woke up. The persistent feelings of sadness began to fade immediately and it felt as though a weight had been lifted.

I was wondering whether it was possible that I really did meet Steve.

A. I don't think you are daft at all. When someone is well known, we may go through a type of mourning for them even though we did not know them in real life. Television brings people right into our homes. They become part of our lives and I know that fans all over the world will have mourned Steve too.

To get back to your question, yes, I do believe that it is possible for the souls of those we do not know to visit us. If we have mourned them they will be aware of our strong feelings of loss and may choose to reassure us that they are safe and well in much the same way that our own loved ones do. I have several case studies involving this phenomenon.

(See also Chapter 10: Celebrities and the Afterlife Experience.)

CHAPTER 14

Is There a Heaven?
Ideas for Further Research and Investigation

*Man is the only animal that contemplates death,
and also the only animal that shows any sign of
doubt of its finality.*

WILLIAM ERNEST HOCKING (1873–1966)

We often find it hard to accept things unless we have either experienced them personally or we have 'scientific proof' that they exist. Of course, the problem here is that our scientific instruments cannot measure everything. And we don't have instruments to measure a great many things we don't understand – yet!

'Proof' in the paranormal is moving forward at a rapid rate, though. Today's mystery is tomorrow's scientifically proven truth. And many areas of soul existence have been studied at length by experts, including doctors and scientists.

You might be interested in reading further about specific areas, so here are some of my favourite subjects, together with suggestions for further reading. You may be able to get the books from your local library, the Internet or specialist book shops. Try doing a special order with your local book shop. Discontinued books often still turn up from time to time on online auction sites and in charity shops, so it's worth persisting if you are interested in tracking something down.

DOES THE SOUL EXIST?

To enable us to believe that there can be communication after the death of the physical body, we need to agree that the soul does actually exist. Its existence has not yet been scientifically 'proven' to the satisfaction of all, but then its non-existence hasn't been proven either.

Our human minds are poor judges of the existence of the soul. We are constantly filtering information down through our basic and limited human senses. And we cannot feel or see the soul, so how can it exist? we ask ourselves. A real conundrum! But why do we even have a word for the soul if there is no such thing? It's worth thinking about, right?

There is a whole world of research concerning the soul and the afterlife – way more than can be covered in my one little book. But here are a few starting points...

Are you sure the afterlife doesn't exist?

Dr Victor Zammit is so sure that the afterlife exists that he has put up $1,000,000 to any sceptic (or anybody else) who can prove that it does *not* exist. Dr Zammit is a former solicitor of the Supreme Court of New South Wales and the High Court of Australia. He is also the author of the book *A Lawyer Presents the Case for the Afterlife: Irrefutable Objective Evidence*. His website is a cornucopia of information about the afterlife and is regularly updated with news about the subject. You can visit it at: www.victorzammit.com.

Hypnotic regression, gateway to an existence between lives

Dr Michael Newton

Dr Newton has undertaken the most amazing research into the journey of the soul after death. I had the pleasure of meeting him in London following a lecture he gave and his work has influenced my own a great deal.

A former clinical hypnotherapist with a private practice, Dr Newton once inadvertently used a trigger word with a patient who then began recalling a heavenly life – a life *between* lives, if you will – whilst under deep hypnosis. His incredible book *Journey of Souls* (Llewellyn Publications, 1994) covers the fascinating line of enquiry that followed this first case. Patients under deep hypnosis recalled previous lives and learning which took place both in heaven and

Earth with their 'soul groups', family members and close friends with whom they seemed to reincarnate over and over again.

Strangely, taking people through their previous bodily death didn't seem to be difficult for them, whilst birth into a new human body seemed much more unattractive! Apparently no one really enjoys being born, but death doesn't appear to be a problem! Upon leaving the body many souls remember that they are 'a soul, not a body' and happily return to their natural state.

Dr Newton's fascinating work seems to show the very reason for life itself, but he is not alone in this work. Others around the world, working independently, seem to have uncovered similar results. If this idea excites you, then I highly recommend Dr Newton's book as a great place to start further investigation.

…and Dolores Cannon

Want more on this subject? I particularly enjoyed Dolores Cannon's book *Between Death and Life* (Gateway Books, 2003) and recommend her *Conversations with a Spirit* (Ozark Mountain Publishers, 1993) too.

The near-death experience

With advances in medical science, many more people are living on after being pronounced physically dead. Others are brought back from the very brink. Classic near-death experiences (NDEs) are happening to people all over the world, both male and female, of all ages and from many different religious backgrounds.

At the point of physical death the person will often hear that they have been pronounced dead. Yet there is also an awareness that they *cannot* be dead because they know what is going on around them. Many will then feel their soul or spirit lift from the physical body. It is common for them to be able to look down upon their 'dead' body at this time before being drawn towards a tunnel with a white light, or 'the God light' at the end.

On reaching the end of the tunnel, the soul usually sees a barrier of some sort – a gate, river, door, wall, etc. – which they must not cross. (It is commonly thought that crossing the barrier means permanent physical death.) Often at this point they will see a deceased relative or even several loved ones. They will tell them that it is 'not their time' and the person will find themselves being pulled back into their physical body, only to find that doctors and nurses are busily working on them, trying to bring them back to life.

Anyone who has been through a near-death experience will most certainly believe in the existence of the soul – they've already taken a journey they will never forget!

Barbara shared this experience with me:

'Not your time'

My dad's sister Lillian was a truly wonderful good and kind soul who never married and had children of her own as she had dedicated her life to looking after her parents. I always thought of her as my 'second mum'. Every Mother's Day I sent her a card and flowers too, because I didn't want her to feel in any way left out. I loved her very much – and still do.

Aunty Lillian had a rare type of blood disorder and when she was ill in hospital she was given too much medication and was left in a coma. I was actually with her when she woke. The whole time she had been in the coma she said she had been in a beautiful garden. She explained to me that she had seen a very bright light and both of her parents holding out their hands to her. She told me that she almost touched them before coming back into her body because it wasn't 'her time'.

Lillian always swore that the experience was real and the doctors later confirmed that they had briefly 'lost her'.

Dr Raymond Moody

One of the earliest people to report on the near-death experience was Dr Raymond Moody in his now classic book *Life after Life* (Stackpole Books, 1976). After over 30 years this book is still in print. I remember reading it as a teenager and it certainly made me look differently at the world around me.

Dannion Brinkley

I also loved *Saved by the Light* by Dannion Brinkley (Villard Books, 1994). Dannion survived a horrific electrocution after the telephone on which he was talking was struck by lightning. He was physically dead for over 20 minutes and during this time he went on an extraordinary visit to a spiritual realm, even meeting angels and being given predictions for the world before he was brought back to his body to continue his life on Earth.

A trip to your local book shop will probably bring forth many more books on the near-death experience.

What we can learn from the near-death experiences of others

Kenneth Ring, PhD, and Evelyn Elsaesser Valarino take the NDE to the next level in their book *Lessons from the Light: What We Can Learn from the Near-Death Experience* (Moment Point Press, Inc., 2000). By looking at the messages and lessons that others have brought back from their close encounters with death we can learn about the after life without having to go through the experience ourselves personally. One of the extraordinary experiences is covered briefly in Chapter 1.

The out-of-body experience

The out-of-body experience (OBE) is the close cousin of the NDE. The first part of the journey can be similar in that people find themselves outside the physical body, but here the similarity usually ends.

An OBE can occur for no obvious reason, but is more likely to occur when the body is extremely tired but the mind is excited or traumatized (causing a sort of separation), during bodily stress, during deep meditation or as part of a dream experience. It can also occur during an illness or accident.

A person experiencing an OBE might find themselves floating around the house or even into other realms. Some people have been able to 'listen in' on conversations happening many miles away and then later report back to the people on whom they eavesdropped! Some people have even seen deceased loved ones during OBEs.

Robert A. Monroe

If you want to learn more about out-of-body experiences then you might enjoy the work of the late Robert Monroe.

When this ordinary family man began having spontaneous out-of-body experiences he was more than a little alarmed. Leaving his body on a regular basis, he found himself visiting places outside our physical realms. In his book *Journeys Out of the Body* (Souvenir Press, 1972) he shares his remarkable travels.

Kathie Jordan

At the age of three Kathie Jordan saw her recently deceased brother Troy at the end of her bed. Between the ages of seven and 22 she was regularly visited by him. He would lift her out of her physical body and escort her to heaven, where she was taught the meaning of life. During her travels she met spiritual teachers, including Jesus himself.

Kathie's story is one of the most fascinating that I have ever read. She shares her experiences in her book *The Birth Called Death* (White Cloud Press, 2003).

Jacky Newcomb

In my own book *An Angel Saved my Life* (ThorsonsElement, 2006) I explored the out-of-body experience for myself. Following a spontaneous OBE of my own, I went on a hilarious spiritual journey in an attempt to repeat the experience. I'm happy to say I succeeded!

PROOF OF LIFE AFTER DEATH?

The work of Dr Gary Schwartz

At the University of Arizona, scientists have carried out research that they believe proves that there is an existence beyond our physical bodies. Dr Gary Schwartz is a Harvard-trained doctor who has worked in laboratory conditions with top mediums such as Allison Dubois, a psychic legal investigator and the subject of the hit show *Medium*, and John Edward, who hosts his own popular television show *Crossing Over*.

Dr Schwartz carried out tests using what he called 'hits and misses'. Staff would compare readings in which the mediums were separated by a screen from the people they read for. No visual clues therefore existed to assist them in bringing messages from the other side.

Staff were said to be amazed at how each of the mediums would bring similar messages from the same deceased people. The results were way beyond coincidental guesses, with what the scientists suggested was between 80 and 90 per cent accuracy.

If you want to learn more about this fascinating work, you can read Dr Schwartz's book *The Afterlife Experiments* (Simon & Schuster, 2002).

Afterlife communication with the Scole Group

Members of an afterlife investigation group at Scole in Norfolk carried out a five-year study into life after death. During the course of their research, messages and symbols appeared on factory-sealed photographic film, objects materialized and disappeared and the spirit communicators themselves gave instructions on how to make devices to exchange messages with the other side.

The group invited engineers, psychologists and even an astrophysicist to observe and test their methods. The book of their investigation, *The Scole Experiment* by Grant and Jane Solomon and Arthur J. Ellison (Piatkus Books, 1999), is extraordinary!

Spontaneous afterlife communication

I am fascinated by positive paranormal experiences and have included some, together with life-saving and life-changing angel experiences, in my books *An Angel Saved my Life* and *An Angel by my Side* (both ThorsonsElement, 2006).

In one chapter of *An Angel Saved my Life,* I investigate the story of Anne, a family friend who died very tragically and unexpectedly in her early fifties. I believe that her sudden death was as much a shock to her as it was to the rest of the village where she worked as a caring dental receptionist. After she passed over, her partner, friends and family all had numerous spontaneous afterlife visitation experiences. Anne seemed particularly good at visiting people in dreams and I even had a visit from her myself. What is especially interesting about this is that even now she still visits regularly and even visits readers of my book!

What I love about this case is that it shows how people on the other side can tune in when we think about them – even strangers and celebrities who are unknown to us!

Past lives

Have you lived before? Probably yes, and most likely hundreds of lifetimes in hundreds of bodies. Research into past-life recall is reaching fever pitch, with some researchers claiming that they have proved reincarnation. Reincarnation, the returning of the soul through many lives, is a belief system of many of the world's peoples, including Native Americans, Hindus and Buddhists. All around the world, there are people who spontaneously recall a previous life or lives on Earth.

Young children are especially fascinating subjects. Pre-school children around the world have unprompted memories of 'when I was big' and 'when I was the mummy and you were the child'. If this area of study interests you, I can recommend *Children Who Have Lived Before* by Trutz Hardo (C. W. Daniel, 2001).

A friend of mine was driving out into the country with her young child one day when the little girl became panic-stricken. 'That's where I used to live with my other mummy,' she said. The traffic was bad and my friend couldn't stop the car, but the child persisted. 'I fell off the tractor and died and then I was born again and came to live with you.'

My friend said she tried desperately to turn the car around, but was never able to find the house again.

New lives

When we lose a loved one it is possible that they might reincarnate back into the same family. In December 2004 a BBC Radio current affairs programme reported on the case of Nathan, whose family believe he is the reincarnation of his own great grandfather. Before he was born a member of the family had a dream announcing his return to them and then Nathan arrived with a birthmark in exactly the same place as that of his great grandfather. As he grew up, he also seemed to have an extraordinary knowledge of local places.

If you are interested in finding out about souls who return to their previous family, you might enjoy the book *Return from Heaven: Beloved Relatives Reincarnated within your Family* by Carol Bowman (HarperCollins, 2001). She has a wonderful story about a young mother, Kathy, whose two-year-old son James died from a cancer above his right ear. His dying words were to tell his mother not to cry for him. Several years later Kathy was with a new partner and had another son, Chad. Right away, she noticed a strange scar-like mark in the same place that James had had his tumour. The doctors dismissed it as a 'birthmark'. But at the age of four Chad began to 'remember things' and one day asked his mother if she remembered their 'other' house. He began to describe the furniture and decoration of a house he had never lived in and recalled toys that had in fact belonged to his deceased brother James. He asked if they could return to the house so that he could collect 'his' toys.

Because of her grief and her promise not to cry, Kathy had not talked about her late son to her new family and had no pictures of the interior of the home that Chad 'remembered' so well. It's a real mystery!

A BEGINNING, NOT AN END

During my own journey I've experienced enough to know that the afterlife is real. We do continue to exist after we die. For many years we've had to rely on faith alone, but now things have changed. Are the veils between our worlds thinning or is it just that our creator himself (or herself) has decided it's time for us to have a deeper understanding of who we are?

The end of our physical life is very much a beginning, not an end, and I hope you will feel that this book is too. I have tried to give you a taster of the mystical and paranormal side of death, but there is so much more just waiting to be discovered. Science fiction is quickly becoming science fact.

Have you lost someone close to you? If so, I hope that you, like me, are lucky enough to experience spontaneous loving communication from the other side, and whatever form it takes, remember that loving energy doesn't change. So Grandma might still be kind and Granddad is probably still grumpy (but at least now he'll apologize for it), while

Dad is still as funny and sweet as he always was. They visit because they want you to know that they still exist and that they are safe and well. They love you and they're proud of you.

Love is love, on both sides of life, and love never dies…

Further Information

I hope this book is just the beginning of a lifetime of interest for you. To help you find your own pathway through the maze of information about afterlife phenomena, here are some starting points:

My own website

> www.jackynewcomb.com – information about me and my work, links and articles about spontaneous afterlife communication, and an online shop selling signed copies of my books and other related products

Psychic protection

> Ted Andrews, *Psychic Protection: Beginnings*, Dragonhawk Publishing, 1998

> Cassandra Eason, *Psychic Protection: Lifts the Spirit*, Foulsham, 2001

Spiritualism

> www.helenduncan.org.uk – information about the celebrated medium the late Helen Duncan

Afterlife existence

www.SurvivalAfterDeath.org – news and articles about mediumship, psi and survival after death

www.museumoftalkingboards.com – for information about the history of spirit boards

www.victorzammit.com – the website of Victor Zammit, author of the book *A Lawyer Presents the Case for the Afterlife*

Bereavement

Darcie D. Sims, PhD, CHT, CT, GMS, is a bereaved parent and child, a grief management specialist, a nationally certified thanatologist, a certified pastoral bereavement specialist and a licensed psychotherapist and hypnotherapist. She is also one of the experts I consulted for this book. She co-authored *A Place for Me: A Healing Journey for Grieving Kids, Footsteps Through Grief, The Other Side of Grief* and *Finding Your Way Through Grief* with her daughter, Alicia Sims Franklin. Darcie also co-authored *The Crying Book* with Bob Baugher. She is an internationally recognized speaker and was coping editor for *Bereavement* magazine for 15 years. She now writes for *Grief Digest*. She can be contacted at GriefInc@aol.com or by calling (253) 929-0649. Visit her website at www.GriefInc.com.

Men's grief

Thomas Golden, LCSW, is well known in the field of healing from loss. His book *Swallowed by a Snake: The Gift of the Masculine Side of Healing* (Golden Healing Publications, 1997) has been acclaimed by the grief specialist Elisabeth Kübler-Ross and others. Tom enjoys presenting workshops in the United States, Canada and Australia, and was named the 1999 International Grief Educator by the Australian Centre for Grief Education. His workshops are known to be entertaining and informative.

Tom brings a gentle sense of humour and a gift for storytelling to his work and draws on his 25 years of practical hands-on clinical experience. His work has been featured in *The New York Times*, *The Washington Post* and *U.S. News and World Report*, as well as on CNN and CBS Evening News. For information on workshops, see Tom's award-winning website, webhealing.com.

The Child Death Helpline
Tel: 0800 282986
Website: www.childdeathhelpline.org.uk
Offers telephone helpline support weekdays from
10 a.m. to 1 p.m. and 7 p.m. to 10 p.m., and weekends
from 7 p.m. to 10 p.m.

The Compassionate Friends
Tel: 0117 953 9639
Website: www.tcf.org.uk
A national organization offering support and friendship
to bereaved parents and families.

Cruse Bereavement Care
Tel: 0870 167 1677 (adult helpline); 0808 808 1677
(young people's helpline)
Website: www.crusebereavementcare.org.uk
A national voluntary organization that offers a free
confidential bereavement counselling service to people
of all ages.

Net Doctor
Website: www.netdoctor.co.uk
Articles about grief and bereavement.

Samaritans
Tel: 0345 909090
Website: www.samaritans.org.uk

Look, Mum, I'm a Butterfly

Look, Mum, I'm a butterfly,
I'm the stars in the sky,
I cannot die.

Watch me, now I'm free,
Look and see.

Hey, Mum, I'm the stars in the sky,
I can even fly.

Listen, Mum, I'm the air that you breathe,
I'm the birds in the trees,
I'm the flowers and the seeds.

Look, Mum, I'm deep in your heart,
We're never apart,
I'm all around.

Look, Mum, I'm a butterfly,
I'm the stars in the sky,
I cannot die.

JACKY NEWCOMB

Titles of Related Interest

We hope you enjoyed this Hay House book.
If you would like to receive a free catalogue featuring additional
Hay House books and products, or if you would like information
about the Hay Foundation, please contact:

Hay House UK Ltd
292B Kensal Rd • London W10 5BE
Tel: (44) 20 8962 1230; Fax: (44) 20 8962 1239
www.hayhouse.co.uk

***

Published and distributed in the United States of America by:
Hay House, Inc. • PO Box 5100 • Carlsbad, CA 92018-5100
Tel.: (1) 760 431 7695 or (1) 800 654 5126;
Fax: (1) 760 431 6948 or (1) 800 650 5115
www.hayhouse.com

Published and distributed in Australia by:
Hay House Australia Ltd • 18/36 Ralph St • Alexandria NSW 2015
Tel.: (61) 2 9669 4299; Fax: (61) 2 9669 4144
www.hayhouse.com.au

Published and distributed in the Republic of South Africa by:
Hay House SA (Pty) Ltd • PO Box 990 • Witkoppen 2068
Tel./Fax: (27) 11 467 8904 • www.hayhouse.co.za

Published and distributed in India by:
Hay House Publishers India • Muskaan Complex • Plot No.3
B-2 • Vasant Kunj • New Delhi – 110 070.
Tel.: (91) 11 41761620; Fax: (91) 11 41761630.
www.hayhouse.co.in

Distributed in Canada by:
Raincoast • 9050 Shaughnessy St • Vancouver, BC V6P 6E5
Tel.: (1) 604 323 7100; Fax: (1) 604 323 2600

***

Sign up via the Hay House UK website to receive the Hay House
online newsletter and stay informed about what's going on with
your favourite authors. You'll receive bimonthly announcements
about discounts and offers, special events, product highlights,
free excerpts, giveaways, and more!
www.hayhouse.co.uk